Once a Catholic

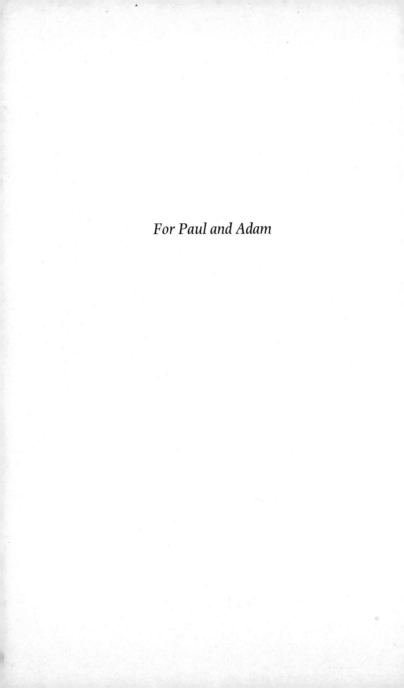

For Paul and Adam

Mary O'Malley

Once a Catholic

Amber Lane Press

All rights whatsoever in this play are strictly reserved
and application for professional or amateur performance
should be made before rehearsals begin to:
Alan Brodie Representation
211 Piccadilly
London W1J 9HF

No performance may be given unless a licence has been obtained.

First published in 1978, reprinted in 2004 by
Amber Lane Press Ltd
Church Street, Charlbury, Oxon OX7 3PR
Telephone: 01608 810024
E-mail: info@amberlanepress.co.uk

Printed and bound in Great Britain by
Creative Print and Design Group, Harmondsworth and Ebbw Vale

ISBN: 0 906399 01 7

Once a Catholic received its world premiere at the Royal Court Theatre, London, on August 10, 1977. It was directed by Mike Ockrent and designed by Poppy Mitchell, with the following cast from the English Stage Company:

MOTHER PETER	Pat Heywood
MOTHER BASIL	Jeanne Watts
MOTHER THOMAS AQUINAS	Doreen Keogh
MR EMANUELLI	John Boswall
FATHER MULLARKEY	John Rogan
MARY MOONEY	Jane Carr
MARY MCGINTY	June Page
MARY GALLAGHER	Anna Keaveney
MARY O'GRADY	Kim Clifford
MARY HENNESSY	Lilian Rostkowska
MARY MURPHY	Sally Watkins
MARY FLANAGAN	Rowena Roberts
DEREK	Daniel Gerroll
CUTHBERT	Mike Grady

Characters

MOTHER THOMAS AQUINAS: A tall, thin, fairly young and very refined Irish nun with spectacles. Headmistress of the Convent of Our Lady of Fatima.

MOTHER PETER: A tall, fat, middle-aged Irish teaching nun.

MOTHER BASIL: A short, fat, elderly Irish teaching nun.

MARY MOONEY: A 5th-former. She is plain and scruffy and has ginger hair, freckles and a very good soprano singing voice.

MARY MCGINTY: A well-developed, blonde and pretty 5th-former.

MARY GALLAGHER: A sensible, attractive, dark-haired 5th-former.

FATHER MULLARKEY: An Irish Priest.

MR EMANUELLI: A very old Music Master, non-specifically foreign. He has white hair down to his shoulders, a bandage on one leg, two walking sticks and a baritone voice.

DEREK: A tall, thin Teddy boy in his late teens.

CUTHBERT: A Catholic 6th-former with a fairly bad case of acne.

Pupils of Form 5A

MARY O'GRADY	MARY MURPHY
MARY HENNESSY	MARY FLANAGAN

The play is set in the Convent of Our Lady of Fatima – a Grammar School for Girls, and in and around the streets of Willesden and Harlesden, London NW10, from September 1956 to July 1957.

ACT ONE

SCENE ONE

[*The Chapel.* FATHER MULLARKEY *is officiating at Morning Mass assisted by* CUTHBERT *dressed as an altar boy.* MR EMANUELLI *is on the organ and the congregation consists of* MOTHER THOMAS AQUINAS, MOTHER PETER, MOTHER BASIL, MARY MOONEY, MARY MCGINTY, MARY GALLAGHER *and the* MEMBERS OF FORM 5A.]

CONGREGATION: [*singing*] 'Qui cum Patre et Filio simul adoratur, et conglorificatur: qui locutus est per Prophetas. Et unam sanctam catholicam et apostolicam Ecclesiam. Confiteor unum baptisma in remissionem peccatorum. Et exspecto resurrectionem mortuorum. Et vitam venturi saeculi. Amen.'

> [FATHER MULLARKEY *kisses the altar and turns to the congregation.*]

FATHER MULLARKEY: 'Dominus vobiscum.'

CONGREGATION: 'Et cum spiritu tuo.'

FATHER MULLARKEY: [*turning back to the altar*] 'Oremus.'

SCENE TWO

[*The Classroom. The girls of Form 5A are at their desks.* MOTHER PETER *walks on carrying some books and a brown paper parcel.*]

GIRLS: Good morning, Mother Peter.

MOTHER PETER: Good morning, 5A. [*She makes the Sign of the Cross.*]

MOTHER PETER *and* GIRLS: In the name of the Father and of the Son and of the Holy Ghost, Amen. Oh Jesus through the most pure heart of Mary I offer thee all the prayers, works and sufferings of this day for all the intentions of thy divine heart. [*She makes the Sign of the Cross again.*] In the name of the Father and of the Son and of the Holy Ghost, Amen.

[MOTHER PETER *sits down and opens the register.*]

MOTHER PETER: [*reading the names rapidly*]

Mary Brennan
Mary Clancy
Mary Delaney
Mary Fahy
Mary Flanagan
Mary Gallagher
Mary Hennessy
Mary Hogan
Mary Kelly
Mary Keogh
Mary Looney
Mary Mooney
Mary McGettigan
Mary McGinty
Mary McGuinness
Mary McHugh
Mary McLoughlin
Mary McManahon
Mary Murphy
Mary Nolan
Mary O'Connor
Mary O'Driscoll
Mary O'Gorman
Mary O'Grady
Mary O'Malley
Mary O'Rourke
Mary O'Shea

Mary O'Toole
Mary Walsh
Mary Whelan
Maria Zajaczkowski

[MOTHER PETER *gets up from her desk.*]

MOTHER PETER: Now. Who's going to tell me what day it is to-day? Mary Mooney?

MARY MOONEY: It's Tuesday, Mother Peter.

MOTHER PETER: Oh, sit down, you little simpleton and think before you speak. Will somebody with a bit of sense please tell me what day it is today? [*Long pause.*] Well? Doesn't the eighth of September ring a bell? A very important bell indeed? [*Pause.*] Evidently it does not. Oh, aren't you the fine pack of heathens! It's Our Blessed Lady's birthday, that's what day it is. I hope you're all ashamed of yourselves. Just imagine how insulted Our Lady must be feeling. Go into the chapel every one of you at dinner time and beg for her forgiveness. Is this an example of the standard I can expect from form 5A this year? I hope you realise that this is the most crucial year of your academic life. In January you'll be sitting the mock O-level exams. And in June the O-levels proper. And I don't intend to have any failures in my form. Any girl showing signs of imbecility will be sent straight down to 5B. And see will that get you to Oxford or Cambridge. Of course, nobody ever passed any exam of their own accord. Only prayer will get results. The best thing each one of you can do is to pick out a particular saint and pray to him or her to get you through. Your Confirmation saint, perhaps, or any saint you fancy. But not St Peter the Apostle, if you wouldn't mind. He's my saint, so he is, and don't any of you go annoying him now. We've a great

understanding, myself and Peter. He's never let me
down in all the years I've been beseeching him for
favours. Oh, he's a wonderful man and a glorious
martyr. I'm mad about him. There are plenty of
other saints who'll be happy to intercede for you.
Indeed, you've a choice of five thousand and more.
From St Aaron the Hermit to St Zoticus the Roman
Martyr. And, you know, there are lots of other
St Peters apart from the real St Peter. A hundred
and thirty-three of them altogether. St Peter of
Nicodemia, St Peter Gonzalez, St Peter the Ven-
erable, St Peter Pappacarbone. And a big batch
of Chinese and Japanese St Peters. So take your
pick of them. Now you must be prepared for a
heavy burden of homework all this year. At least
three hours every evening. Plus revision. And
double that amount at the weekend. If any girl
has ideas about delivering papers or serving behind the counter of a Woolworth on a Saturday
she can put such ideas right out of her head.
Under no circumstances will Mother Thomas
Aquinas give permission for a girl from Our Lady
of Fatima to take on a job of work. And anyway,
your parents have a duty to provide you with
sufficient pocket money. They also have a duty
to supply you with the correct school uniform,
which must be obtained from Messrs Houlihan
and Hegarty and only Messrs Houlihan and
Hegarty. There's no greater insult to this school
than to see a girl dressed up in a shoddy imita-
tion of the uniform. Mary Mooney, step up here
to me and face the class.

> [MARY MOONEY *comes forward and stands next to*
> MOTHER PETER*'s desk. She is wearing a large, shape-*

[*less hand-knitted cardigan and a thick pair of striped, knitted knee-length socks.*]

Will you look at this girl's cardigan! Who knitted you that monstrosity, Mary Mooney?

MARY MOONEY: My mother, Mother Peter.

MOTHER PETER: Did she now? Have you no school cardigan to wear?

MARY MOONEY: No, Mother Peter.

MOTHER PETER: Will you please inform your mother that she must order you two school cardigans from Houlihan and Hegarty immediately. And don't dare come into school wearing that thing again.

MARY MOONEY: No, Mother. Sorry, Mother.

[MARY MOONEY *goes off.*]

MOTHER PETER: Come back here a minute.

[MARY MOONEY *comes back.*]

Mary Mooney, have you joined a football team?

MARY MOONEY: No, Mother.

MOTHER PETER: Well, what are those horrible socks doing on your feet? Is this another example of your mother's handiwork?

MARY MOONEY: Yes, Mother.

MOTHER PETER: God help the girl. Isn't her mother a martyr for the knitting. Go back to your place now and don't ever let me see you wearing socks like that again.

MARY MOONEY: No, Mother. Sorry, Mother.

[MARY MOONEY *goes off.* MOTHER PETER *opens the brown paper parcel and holds up a thick pair of long-legged bloomers.*]

MOTHER PETER: Now you all know what this is, don't you? It's the Our Lady of Fatima knicker and it's the only type of knicker we want to see worn at this school. An increasing number of girls have been leaving off this knicker and coming to school in . . . in scanty bits of things that wouldn't cover the head of a leprechaun and showing them off under their PE shorts. Hands up any girl who has on a knicker like this. Is that all? Hands up every girl who has a knicker like this at home. And why haven't you got them on you, that's what I'd like to know. Oh, aren't you the brazen little madams. You know well there's a man out in the garden. A man who has to walk up and down with his wheelbarrow right past the tennis courts. Mary Gallagher, come right up here to me and give out two knickers to every girl who hasn't any. I'll collect the cash first thing tomorrow morning.

[MARY GALLAGHER *gives out the knickers.*]

Well now, let us turn our attention to Our Lady on the occasion of her birthday. No woman on this earth was ever worthy of the holy name of Mary. The Mother of God is elevated high above all other human creatures. Because of the special privileges given to her by God. Mary Murphy, will you name one of Our Lady's special privileges.

MARY MURPHY: The Immaculate Conception, Mother Peter.

MOTHER PETER: Yes indeed. Every ordinary baby comes into the world with a stain upon its soul. The big, black stain of original sin. But Our Lady came into the world with a soul of sparkling white. Because the Mother of Jesus had to be immaculate. Immaculate through and through. Mary Mooney, who were Our Lady's parents?

MARY MOONEY: I'm sorry, Mother Peter. I can't remember.

MOTHER PETER: You can't remember the names of Our Lady's parents? Why can't you?

MARY MOONEY: I don't know, Mother Peter.

MOTHER PETER: Mary Gallagher, will you enlighten this irreligious girl.

MARY GALLAGHER: Our Lady's mother was St Anne, Mother Peter. And Our Lady's father was St Joachim.

MOTHER PETER: Quite correct. It's a very great pity we don't know more about the lives of St Anne and St Joachim. Indeed we know nothing at all about either one of them. But they must have been two of the holiest saints that ever walked the earth. Mary Mooney, tell your mother you'll be late home from school tomorrow evening. You'll be staying behind to write out the names of Our Lady's parents one hundred times. And I want to see the lines written out in a legible hand. The same applies to all work handed in to me. I hope you each have your very own fountain pen. If you haven't then you must go out and get one. And I'll tell you what you must do when you get the pen home. Take a clean sheet of paper and write on it the holy names of Jesus, Mary and Joseph. Then throw the sheet of paper into the fire. That way the pen will never let you down. Mary O'Grady, will you tell me another of Our Lady's special privileges?

MARY O'GRADY: The Assumption, Mother Peter.

MOTHER PETER: Correct. At the completion of her life on earth Our Lady did not die. Our Lady was assumed into Heaven. Taken straight up, body and soul, to reign as Queen in everlasting glory. The Mother of God could not be subjected to such an indignity as death. Death and corruption in the coffin are part of the penalty of original sin, and the rest of us will have to wait until the end of the world when we'll all rise again on the Last Day of Judgement to be finally re-united with our bodies. What is it, Mary Flanagan?

MARY FLANAGAN: Please Mother Peter. If somebody loses a leg on earth will he get it back on the Day of Judgement?

MOTHER PETER: Indeed he will. And he'll get a higher place in Heaven into the bargain. Provided he's been a good man on earth. Mary McGinty?

MARY MCGINTY: Please Mother, will the souls in Hell get their bodies back at the end of the world?

MOTHER PETER: Oho, they most certainly will. They'll be brought up for the Day of Judgement with the rest of us. And when their wickedness has been revealed to the whole of mankind they'll go back down to Hell taking their bodies with them into the everlasting fire. And remember, no sin ever goes unrecorded. Every little lapse will be brought to judgement. And not just your actual deeds. But every iniquitous thought that was ever carried inside your head will be revealed. And the sinner will stand alone and be shamed in front of family, friends, neighbours, teachers, and every member of the human race. [*Pause.*] Well now, 5A, we've a hard year's work ahead of us. But there are nevertheless a number of treats in store. Mother Basil has one of her fillum shows planned, the sixth form will be giving us another operetta in the summer, and this year you'll all have a chance to be in the chorus. But the most exciting event of all will be in the Easter holidays. When we'll be taking a party of girls away on a pilgrimage. A very special pilgrimage to Fatima. What do you think of that now? Isn't it wonderful news? We'll be sending the full information out to your parents later on, and I'm sure they'll all be happy to make a financial sacrifice in order to give you the benefit of this splendid opportunity. And now we'd better have some nominations for the election of a captain of the form.

SCENE THREE

[*The Canteen.* MARY MCGINTY *and* MARY GALLAGHER *are sitting at a table.* MOTHER BASIL *is pacing up and down.* MARY GALLAGHER *is laboriously eating a plate of rice pudding. She has an empy dinner plate in front of her.* MARY MCGINTY *is still struggling through her dinner.*]

MOTHER BASIL: Mary McGinty, will you stop playing about with that stew and eat it up properly.

MARY MCGINTY: I can't swallow the meat, Mother Basil.

MOTHER BASIL: Oh, isn't it a pity for you? Why don't you try opening your mouth and see if that will help you at all?

MARY MCGINTY: There's great big lumps of gristle in this meat, Mother Basil.

MOTHER BASIL: There's no gristle in that meat, is there Mary Gallagher? You don't realise how lucky you are. Think of all the poor black fellows dropping down dead in the heart of Africa for want of a bit of stewing steak. Look at Mary Gallagher. She's finished all hers and is eating her pudding up nicely.

MARY GALLAGHER: Please may I leave this last little bit, Mother Basil?

MOTHER BASIL: You may not! Eat every single bit and offer it up for all the souls in Purgatory. Come on now. Think of each grain of rice as a poor soul in agony. And remember an hour in Purgatory is as long as a cen-

tury on earth. As you swallow every mouthful just
imagine all the souls you're getting a bit of remis-
sion for. Oh, come on and eat it up! Will you eat it!
[*She stamps her foot.*] Oh, damn the two of yeez with
your fussing and finicking. D'you think I have all
day to be standing here? Well I haven't. I've a lot of
things to do. A lot of very important things. D'you
hear me?

MARY GALLAGHER: I've finished it, Mother.

MOTHER BASIL: All right. Go on and get out of it.

[MARY GALLAGHER *goes off.*]

Come on now, Mary McGinty. Eat it up or I . . . I . . .
I . . . I . . . I'm not going to stand for any more of this
old nonsense.

MARY MCGINTY: Please Mother, I think I'm going to be sick.

MOTHER BASIL: Ah! Puke away then. Go on and be as sick as
you like. But you'll stay behind and clear it all up
after you.

MARY MCGINTY: I just can't eat it, Mother. I can't. I honestly
can't.

MOTHER BASIL: You can't? You mean you won't. Well you will!
Give me that knife and fork!

MARY MCGINTY: I'm eating it, Mother. I'm eating it.

MOTHER BASIL: That's the idea. Keep it up now. I'll tell you what
we'll do. Let's see if you can polish it all off in the
time it takes me to say a Hail Holy Queen. Are you
ready now? In the name of the Father and of the Son
and of the Holy Ghost, Amen. Hail Holy Queen,
Mother of Mercy, Hail Our Life, Our Sweetness and
Our Hope. To thee do we cry, poor banished children of Eve. To thee do we send up our sighs, mourn-
ing and weeping in this vale of tears. Turn then,
most gracious advocate, thine eyes of mercy towards

us and after this our exile, show unto us the blessed fruit of thy womb, Jesus. [*She beats her breast three times.*] O clement! O loving! O sweet Virgin Mary! Pray for us O Holy Mother of God ...

MARY MCGINTY: [*nearly choking*] That we may be made worthy of the promises of Christ.

MOTHER BASIL: Good girl.

[MARY MCGINTY *retches.*]

SCENE FOUR

[*The Music Room.* MR EMANUELLI *comes hobbling in with two walking sticks. He sits down at the piano.*]

GIRLS: Good afternoon, Mr Emanuelli.

MR EMANUELLI: What good afternoon? My leg is giving me gip. I am crucified with pain and you tell me good afternoon. It's a rotten afternoon. [*He points with one stick.*] Look at me! Don't look to the left or the right, look straight up here at me, please! Now. [*He sings.*]
'When Jesus Christ was four years old
The angels brought him toys of gold
Which no man ever bought or sold.'
[*He stops singing and points with his stick.*] You! The girl with the frizzly hair. Sing for me! Come on, come on. Stand up and sing it if you please. 'When Jesus Christ ...' [*He gets ready to conduct with his walking stick.*]

MARY FLANAGAN: [*extremely off key*]
'When Jesus Christ was four years old
The angels brought him toys of ...'

MR EMANUELLI: No, no! No, no, no, no, no, no, no, no, no. That is not singing. That is ruddy awful caterwauling. Can you hold in your hand a broom? Well? Can you?

MARY FLANAGAN: Yes, Sir.

MR EMANUELLI: Good. Then you will sweep the stage for my
production of *The Mikado* next July. Look at me!
[*He sings.*]
'And yet with these he would not play
He made him small fow-ow-owl out of clay
And blessed them till they floo-oo-oo-oo-oo-oo-oo
away.
O Laudate domine.'
[*He points with his stick.*] You! The girl with the
glasses. What do you call. National Health. Sing it!

MARY HENNESSY : [*croaking in a very low octave*]
'And yet with these he would not play
He made him small fow-ow-owl . . .'

MR EMANUELLI: Enough! Enough! Where am I? I can't be in the
Convent of Our Lady of Fatima. I must be in the
zoological gardens. At Regent's Park. This voice is
bad. Bad, bad, bad. I will not have such a honking
in my Gilbert and Sullivan chorus. I want a chorus
of Japanese schoolgirls, nobles, guards and coolies
for *The Mikado*. And I need a Nanki-Poo. There is a
shortage of prima donnas in the sixth form. So let
us see who we can find in here. I will not have
second-raters in my productions. You have seen my
Iolanthe, my *HMS Pinafore*, my *Pirates*. You know
what a professional standard I demand. I was once
a professional myself, you know. You have heard
all about my reputation, eh? Psst, psst, psst, psst,
psst. He was a famous opera singer before the 1914-
18 war. You have heard that, eh? You! [*He points
with his stick.*] The little tiny girl. Have you heard
such a rumour about me?

MARY O'GRADY: Yes, Sir.

MR EMANUELLI: It's a fact. I was famous all over the world. But what happened to me, eh? You think you know what happened? Something to do with my leg? Eh? Psst, psst, psst. I wonder what is wrong with Mr Emanuelli's leg. Is it gangrene? Is it gout? Is it a war wound? Whatever it is, it certainly stinks out the music room. Can anyone smell this leg? Well? Speak out! Yes or no?

GIRLS: No, Sir.

MR EMANUELLI: You are all a load of liars because I can ruddy well smell it myself. Look at me!
[*He sings.*]
'Jesus Christ thou child so wise
Bless my hands and fill my eyes.'
[*He points with his stick.*] You! The girl with the ginger hair, lurking low. Sing it!

MARY MOONEY: 'Jesus Christ thou child so wise
Bless my hands and fill my eyes.'

MR EMANUELLI: Again! [*He sings.*]
'And bring my soul to Par-ar-adise
To Par-ar-adise.'

MARY MOONEY: 'And bring my soul to Par-ar-adise
To Par-ar-adise.'

MR EMANUELLI: Yes. Yes, yes, yes, yes. This one is good. Quite good. But I don't believe it. Such a plain young missy. Come here. Come on, come on. Come right up here and let me look at you.

[MARY MOONEY *comes forward.*]

Yes. You will be Nanki-Poo. He is a young man. And you are a boyish-looking girl. Come to see me later. Now go away.

[MARY MOONEY *goes off.*]

We will all sing Jesus Christ together. [*He gets up.*]
My ear is coming close to every mouth. So warble
away and don't let me hear any cacophony. One,
two, three, four.

GIRLS: [*singing*]
'When Jesus Christ was four years old
The angels brought him toys of gold
Which no man ever bought or sold ...'

SCENE FIVE

[*A Street in Harlesden.* MARY MCGINTY, MARY GALLA-
GHER *and* MARY MOONEY *are walking along carry-
ing heavy satchels and eating Mars Bars.* MARY
MCGINTY *has her hat in her hand.*]

MARY GALLAGHER: Put your hat back on, McGinty.

MARY MCGINTY: No. I refuse to walk the streets with a pisspot
on my head. It's bad enough having to wear these
socks and a stupid-looking gymslip.

MARY GALLAGHER: What if a prefect sees you. You'll only get
reported.

MARY MCGINTY: It wouldn't worry me if I got expelled. I wonder what you have to do to get expelled from that
old dump.

MARY GALLAGHER: You could tell them you'd become a member of the pudding club.

MARY MCGINTY: Yeah. Or you could make a big long willy out
of plasticine and stick it on the crucifix in the chapel.

MARY MOONEY: You mustn't say things like that.

MARY MCGINTY: Why not? D'you reckon a thunderbolt is gonna
come hurtling down from Heaven?

MARY MOONEY: It doesn't happen straight away. It happens

when you're least expecting it. You'd better make an Act of Contrition.

MARY MCGINTY: [*looking up*] Sorry, Jesus.

MARY MOONEY: My Dad knows this man who used to be a monk. But he couldn't keep his vows so he asked if he could be released. On the day he left he came skipping down the path with his collar in his hand. And when he opened the monastery gate he saw an alsatian sitting outside. So he hung his collar round the alsatian's neck and went on his way laughing all along the road. After that he started going into pubs every night and boasting to all the people about what he'd gone and done with his collar. Then one day he went and got married. And while he was on his honeymoon he started to get a really bad pain in his back. He was in such a terrible agony he could only walk about with a stoop. And after a while he was completely bent up double. Then he started to lose his voice. He went to loads of different doctors but none of them could do anything to help him. And now he can only get about on all fours. And when he opens his mouth to say anything he barks just like a dog.

MARY GALLAGHER: Is that true?

MARY MOONEY: Yes. He lives in Shepherd's Bush.

MARY MCGINTY: Why can't you keep your stupid old stories to yourself? You're as bad as Mother Peter, you are.

MARY MOONEY: No I am not. Huh. I bet if you were knocked down by a trolleybus this evening you'd be yelling your head off for a priest.

MARY MCGINTY: Oh no I wouldn't.

MARY GALLAGHER: Well I certainly would.

MARY MCGINTY: Oh shit! I was only having a joke about trying to get expelled. I don't even have to get expelled, come to think of it. I'm old enough to go out to work.

MARY GALLAGHER: You wouldn't get much of a job without any qualifications.

[DEREK, *the Teddy boy, comes swaggering along the street behind them.*]

MARY MCGINTY: Huh. I couldn't care less about exams.

MARY GALLAGHER: Well that's the main difference between you and me, McGinty, because I do happen to care.

MARY MOONEY: Yes, and so do 1.

MARY MCGINTY: Huh. There's millions of jobs I could do. [*She sees* DEREK.] Oh blimey!

DEREK: Afternoon, girls. I must say you're looking very smart.

MARY MCGINTY: Leave off. What you doing round here, anyway?

DEREK: Just having a bit of a promenade. You don't mind, do you? Or is this a private road?

MARY MCGINTY: Aren't you supposed to be at work?

DEREK: Had to take the day off, didn't I? Touch of the old neuralgia.

MARY MCGINTY: Don't give me that.

DEREK: Are you calling me a liar, darling?

MARY MCGINTY: No . . .

DEREK: Well just make sure you don't, 'cos nobody accuses me of telling lies. All right? [*He looks over at the other two girls.*] How you doing, girls? [*to* MARY MCGINTY] Ain't you gonna introduce me to your two lovely mates?

MARY MCGINTY: Yeah, well that's Mary Gallagher. And that's Mary Mooney. His name's Derek.

[DEREK *winks and clicks his tongue at them, then he turns back to* MARY MCGINTY.]

DEREK: You gonna be down the White Hart tonight, by any chance?

MARY MCGINTY: I might be.

DEREK: Oh, well, I'll see you inside, then, shall I?

MARY MCGINTY: You've got to be joking. You don't think I'm gonna go wandering in there and have everybody staring at me all on me tod.

DEREK: All right, all right. I'll see you outside then. Half past seven. And you be there, darling. Right?

> [*He clicks his tongue and winks at the other two, then he goes swaggering off.*]

MARY GALLAGHER: Is that your bloke?

MARY MCGINTY: Sort of

MARY GALLAGHER: How long have you been going out with him?

MARY MCGINTY: About two and a half weeks. D'you think he's nice looking?

MARY GALLAGHER: Well . . . he's not exactly my sort of bloke.

MARY MCGINTY: No, well, of course we all know your type, don't we? Smarmy little Catholic schoolboys, with short back and sides. And acne.

MARY GALLAGHER: Cuthbert has not got acne.

MARY MCGINTY: He did have the day I saw him. He had a beautiful crop of blackheads on his boat-race. And he had a load of pimples, all about ready to pop. Ugh!

MARY GALLAGHER: Well at least he's not bow-legged like that long streak of paralysed piss that's just gone by. I wonder where he left his horse.

MARY MCGINTY: Oh, shut your face.

MARY MOONEY: I'd like to know how you're going to get your homework done if you're going to be gadding about all night.

MARY MCGINTY: I was thinking of copying your History on the trolleybus tomorrow morning. And having a lend of Gallagher's Latin after lunch.

MARY GALLAGHER: You've got some nerve.

MARY MCGINTY: I'll do the same for you some time.

MARY GALLAGHER: Oh yes, and pigs might fly.

MARY MCGINTY: [*to* MARY MOONEY] You'd better be waiting for me tomorrow morning at Willesden Green.

MARY MOONEY: All right.

MARY GALLAGHER: And don't forget your knicker money, will you?

MARY MOONEY: I didn't have to have any knickers off Mother Peter.

MARY MCGINTY: Oh, no, you wouldn't, of course. You always wear passion killers, don't you?

MARY MOONEY: You'll be wearing them yourself from tomorrow.

> [MARY MCGINTY *takes a pair of bloomers out of her satchel and puts them over her head.*]

MARY MCGINTY: How's that? She didn't actually say you had to put them on your bum.

> [*They go off.*]

SCENE SIX

[*The Biology Lab.* MOTHER BASIL, *wearing a blood-stained apron, is dissecting a female rabbit.*]

MOTHER BASIL: Now this is the abdomen, which contains the remainder of the alimentary canal together with the organs of excretion and reproduction. The female ova are produced in the two ovaries which you can see here lying behind the kidneys. Close to each ovary there's a Fallopian tube. Each Fallopian tube widens out into an oviduct leading to a uterus, which in turn opens out together with the second uterus, here, into a much larger tube, the vagina.

[*The Angelus bell tolls loudly several times.* MOTHER BASIL *wipes her hands and makes the Sign of the Cross. The 'Hail Mary' part of the following prayer is recited very rapidly indeed.*]

In the name of the Father and of the Son and of the Holy Ghost, Amen. The Angel of the Lord declared unto Mary.

GIRLS: And she conceived of the Holy Ghost.

MOTHER BASIL: Hail Mary full of grace the Lord is with thee. Blessed art thou amongst women and blessed is the fruit of thy womb Jesus.

GIRLS: Holy Mary Mother of God pray for us sinners now and at the hour of our death, Amen.

MOTHER BASIL: Behold the handmaid of the Lord.

GIRLS: Be it done unto me according to thy word.

MOTHER BASIL: Hail Mary full of grace the Lord is with thee. Blessed art thou amongst women and blessed is the fruit of thy womb Jesus.

GIRLS: Holy Mary Mother of God pray for us sinners now and at the hour of our death, Amen.

MOTHER BASIL: And the word was made flesh.

GIRLS: And dwelt amongst us,

MOTHER BASIL: Hail Mary full of grace the Lord is with thee. Blessed art thou amongst women and blessed is the fruit of thy womb Jesus.

GIRLS: Holy Mary Mother of God pray for us sinners now and at the hour of our death, Amen.

MOTHER BASIL: Pray for us O Holy Mother of God.

GIRLS: That we may be made worthy of the promises of Christ.

MOTHER BASIL: Pour forth we beseech thee O Lord thy grace into our hearts that we to whom the Incarnation of Christ thy Son was made known by the message of an Angel, may by his Passion and Cross be brought to the glory of his resurrection through the same Christ Our Lord, Amen. [*Sign of the Cross.*] In the name of the Father and of the Son and of the Holy Ghost, Amen. Now, this organ here, the vagina, at its anal end leads to a much smaller tube, the urethra, which opens to the exterior. As the breeding season approaches the ova will pass down the Fallopian tube through the oviduct and into the uterus. For the purposes of reproduction an enormous number of sperm from the male will be introduced into the vagina. The sperm will swim along the uterus and through the oviduct into the Fallopian tube. Yes, Mary Mooney?

MARY MOONEY: Please Mother Basil, could you tell us how the sperm from the male gets introduced into the vagina?

MOTHER BASIL: What?

MARY MOONEY: Could you tell us how . . .

MOTHER BASIL: I heard what you said, you little madam. Get out of here this minute and stand outside till the lesson is over.

[MARY MOONEY *gets up and goes off.*]

God bless us and save us! I'm going to send that girl upstairs to see Mother Thomas Aquinas. Now. When an ovum has been fertilised it'll be implanted in the uterus where the protective membranes and the placenta will be formed. The dirty little devil! Trying to make a laughing stock out of me! The placenta is the organ by which the embryo is attached to the uterus of the mother. Oh, the cheek of it! Mother Thomas Aquinas will deal with her. This uterus here, by the way, is known as a duplex uterus. I never heard the like of it before! The little trollop! All rabbits and rodents have this type of uterus. There is also the simplex uterus which is found in the higher primates including man, or rather woman, but we don't want to be going into that. A detention is no good to that one. What she wants is a good, hard kick up the behind.

SCENE SEVEN

[MOTHER THOMAS AQUINAS' *Office*. MARY MOONEY *is standing in front of* MOTHER THOMAS AQUINAS' *desk*.]

MOTHER THOMAS AQUINAS: How dare you ask Mother Basil such a precocious question? How dare you?

MARY MOONEY: I'm sorry, Mother Thomas Aquinas, but I didn't know I was asking anything wrong.

MOTHER THOMAS AQUINAS: You didn't know? Are you sure you didn't know?

MARY MOONEY: No, Mother. I mean yes, Mother.

MOTHER THOMAS AQUINAS: In that case you must be an extremely ignorant girl. Is that what you are, Mary Mooney? Ignorant?

MARY MOONEY: I don't know, Mother Thomas Aquinas.

MOTHER THOMAS AQUINAS: Don't you? Hasn't your mother ever had a little chat with you?

MARY MOONEY: Yes Mother. But she doesn't ever chat about rabbits.

MOTHER THOMAS AQUINAS: Never mind the rabbits. Hasn't she ever warned you about boys?

MARY MOONEY: No, Mother Thomas Aquinas.

MOTHER THOMAS AQUINAS: The woman is evidently guilty of neglecting her duties. Such ignorance is inexcusable in a girl of fifteen. I must write to your mother this afternoon and tell her to start instructing you immediately on certain matters. Go along now. And try to be a bit more mature.

MARY MOONEY: Yes, Mother Thomas. Thank you, Mother Thomas. Sorry, Mother Thomas.

SCENE EIGHT

[*The Classroom.* MARY MCGINTY, MARY MOONEY *and* MARY GALLAGHER *are at their desks.*]

MARY MCGINTY: Fancy her not knowing the facts of life.

MARY MOONEY: So what?

MARY MCGINTY: You know a man's willy?

MARY MOONEY: Yes.

MARY MCGINTY: D'you know what it's for?

MARY MOONEY: Yes. For being excused.

[MARY MCGINTY *and* MARY GALLAGHER *exchange looks.*]

MARY GALLAGHER: Yes, well he does do that with it, of course. But he can do something else with it as well.

MARY MCGINTY: Not at the same time, though.

MARY GALLAGHER: No. Did you know he had two balls as well?

MARY MOONEY: Two what?

MARY MCGINTY: Bollocks.

MARY GALLAGHER: And the same to you.

MARY MCGINTY: You know when you get married you have to go to bed with your husband.

MARY MOONEY: No. My Mum and Dad don't.

MARY GALLAGHER: Don't they?

MARY MOONEY: No. My Dad always goes to bed at nine o'clock. Me and my Mum go at ten. After she's finished her packing.

MARY GALLAGHER: Her what?

MARY MOONEY: Well, she gets out all our best dresses and packs them in a suitcase with her real fox fur and her jewellery. Then she gets out her canteen of cutlery and her best bone china tea set and she puts them in with a tin of corned beef and a crucifix.

MARY McGINTY: What for?

MARY MOONEY: In case we have an air raid in the night.

MARY GALLAGHER: I heard the war ended eleven years ago.

MARY MOONEY: Yes, but we have to be ready for the next one. The devil works in threes, don't forget. And this country's got a lot more coming to it for the things it did to Ireland.

MARY GALLAGHER: What things?

MARY MOONEY: Things that'd make your hair stand up on end if only you knew.

MARY GALLAGHER: Such as what?

MARY MOONEY: I don't know. I wasn't there. My Mum was, though.

MARY McGINTY: D'you share a bedroom with your Mum?

MARY MOONEY: Yes. And my Dad.

MARY McGINTY: Bloody hell.

MARY MOONEY: Well, we've only got one bedroom. Me and my Mum have the double bed. And he's got one on his own.

MARY GALLAGHER: Does she ever get in his bed?

MARY MOONEY: No!

MARY MCGINTY: She must have done once.

MARY GALLAGHER: You have to get in bed with your husband to have a baby.

MARY MCGINTY: And they both have to take their pyjamas off.

MARY MOONEY: Oh no! How could they? I'd never do anything so rude.

MARY GALLAGHER: You'll have to if you ever get married. Our Lady was the only one who never had to do it.

MARY MOONEY: Wasn't she lucky?

MARY MCGINTY: It wasn't so lucky for poor old Joseph, though. I reckon he must have used it to stir his tea.

MARY MOONEY: Used what?

MARY MCGINTY: His cock.

MARY GALLAGHER: Prick.

MARY MCGINTY: Dick.

MARY GALLAGHER: Tool.

MARY MCGINTY: Sssh!

> [MOTHER PETER *comes in, gets something out of her desk and goes off.*]

MARY GALLAGHER: When you're expecting a baby you stop having the curse. That's how they can tell.

MARY MOONEY: Are you sure?

MARY GALLAGHER: Yes of course.

MARY MCGINTY: You don't always have to have a baby, though. Not if the man uses a French letter.

MARY GALLAGHER: You often see a used one lying about in the park.

MARY MCGINTY: Yeah. Don't ever sit on the seat in a public toilet.

MARY GALLAGHER: No. just hover over it. In case you get VD.

MARY MCGINTY: Your body breaks out in big sores. And after a while it starts to rot away.

MARY GALLAGHER: I know someone who's had VD. She stands outside Dollis Hill station selling papers. All her nose has been eaten away. She's just got a hole in the middle of her face.

MARY MCGINTY: Cor, I wouldn't buy a paper off her.

MARY MOONEY: My Mum must be having a baby. I know for a fact she's stopped having the curse. I thought it was a bit funny.

MARY GALLAGHER: She must have got in his bed while you were fast asleep.

MARY MOONEY: There isn't enough room for the two of them.

MARY MCGINTY: They don't need all that much room. The man lies on top of the woman.

[MOTHER BASIL *comes in.*]

MOTHER BASIL: Get up this minute and go and take some healthy exercise. Sitting nattering like a bunch of old fish-wives.

[*The girls get up.*]

I'd like to know what all that whispering was about. That's what I'd like to know.

SCENE NINE

[*The Classroom.* MOTHER PETER *is at her desk. Two extra chairs have been placed nearby.*]

MOTHER PETER: Now sit up straight and clear the tops of your desks. Give your answers loud and clear and God help any girl who lets me down.

[FATHER MULLARKEY *makes an entrance with* MOTHER THOMAS AQUINAS.]

GIRLS: Good morning, Father Mullarkey. Good morning, Mother Thomas Aquinas.

FATHER MULLARKEY: Good morning, Mother Peter. Good morning, girls.

[MOTHER PETER *goes to sit on one of the side chairs with* MOTHER THOMAS AQUINAS.]

Have they been working hard, Mother Peter?

MOTHER PETER: Indeed they have, Father.

[*From his pocket* FATHER MULLARKEY *takes a little red booklet:* A Catechism of Christian Doctrine. *Throughout the following scene he flicks through this booklet.*]

And do they know their Catechism?

MOTHER PETER: There's no excuse for any girl who doesn't.

FATHER MULLARKEY: Which girl is the Captain of the form, Mother Peter?

MOTHER PETER: Mary Hennessy is the Captain, Father.

FATHER MULLARKEY: Well now, Mary Hennessy. Stand up and tell me who is the head of the Catholic Church.

MARY HENNESSY: The Pope.

FATHER MULLARKEY: Is that a fact? Are you sure this girl is fit to be the Captain, Mother Peter? Are the duties of leadership so exacting that she hasn't time to study her religion? Sit down, Captain Hennessy, and let the blondy girl over there tell us the answer to the question. Who is the head of the Catholic Church?

MARY FLANAGAN: The head of the Catholic Church is Jesus Christ Our Lord.

FATHER MULLARKEY: And has the Church a visible head on earth?

MARY FLANAGAN: The Church has a visible head on earth. The Bishop of Rome, who is the Vicar of Christ.

FATHER MULLARKEY: What is the Bishop of Rome called?

MARY FLANAGAN: The Bishop of Rome is called the Pope, which word signifies Father.

FATHER MULLARKEY: Make a note of that, Mary Hennessy. And now stand up and tell me: is the Pope infallible?

MARY HENNESSY: The Pope is infallible.

FATHER MULLARKEY: Correct. That girl there. Which are the four sins crying to Heaven for vengeance?

MARY MOONEY: The four sins crying to Heaven for vengeance are Wilful Murder, The Sin of Sodom, Oppression of the Poor and Defrauding Labourers of their Wages.

FATHER MULLARKEY: Is it a great evil to fall into mortal sin?

MARY MOONEY: It is the greatest of all evils to fall into mortal sin.

FATHER MULLARKEY: Why is it called mortal sin?

MARY MOONEY: It is called mortal sin because it kills the soul and deserves Hell.

FATHER MULLARKEY: Now you there with the horse's tail. Is it a mortal sin to neglect to hear Mass on Sundays and Holy Days of Obligation?

MARY MURPHY: It is a mortal sin to neglect to hear Mass on Sundays and Holy Days of Obligation.

FATHER MULLARKEY: Make no mistake about it, there's no greater sin on all this earth than the deliberate missing of Mass. [*He bangs on the desk.*] A person who lies in bed and refuses to get up for Mass is committing a far more serious sin than a man who lashes out and murders his wife in a fit of fury. God would surely be merciful to the man who lost control. But you can't expect God to condone a premeditated decision to stay away from Holy Mass. The blondy girl again. Where is God?

MARY FLANAGAN: God is everywhere.

FATHER MULLARKEY: Had God any beginning?

MARY FLANAGAN: God had no beginning. He always was, He is and He always will be.

FATHER MULLARKEY: Has God any body?

MARY FLANAGAN: God has no body. He is a spirit.

FATHER MULLARKEY: Is there only one God?

MARY FLANAGAN: There is only one God.

FATHER MULLARKEY: Are there three persons in God?

MARY FLANAGAN: There are three persons in God: God the Father, God the Son and God the Holy Ghost

FATHER MULLARKEY: Are these three persons three Gods?

MARY FLANAGAN: These three persons are not three Gods. The Father, the Son and the Holy Ghost are all one and the same God.

FATHER MULLARKEY: Does God know and see all things?

MARY FLANAGAN: God knows and sees all things, even our most secret thoughts.

FATHER MULLARKEY: How are you to know what God has revealed?

MARY FLANAGAN: I am to know what God has revealed by the testimony, teaching and authority of the Catholic Church.

FATHER MULLARKEY: Now then, Captain Hennessy! What is the Sixth Commandment?

MARY HENNESSY: The Sixth Commandment is: 'Thou shalt not commit adultery'.

FATHER MULLARKEY: What does the Sixth Commandment forbid?

MARY HENNESSY: The Sixth Commandment forbids all sins of impurity with another's wife or husband.

FATHER MULLARKEY: Does the Sixth Commandment forbid whatever is contrary to holy purity?

MARY HENNESSY: The Sixth Commandment forbids whatever is contrary to holy purity, in looks, words or actions.

FATHER MULLARKEY: Good. Now I want to say a little word to you about the vital importance of purity. You're all getting to be big girls now. Indeed some of you are bigger than others. Isn't it a great joy to be young and healthy with all your life before you. Sooner or later you might want to share your life with a member of the opposite sex. The best way to find a boyfriend is to join a Catholic Society where you'll have scope for all sorts of social activities. Now when you've met your good Catholic boy and you're getting to know each other he might suggest a bit of a kiss and a cuddle. Well, let him wait. And if he doesn't want to wait let him go. Any cuddling and kissing is bound to arouse bad feelings and desires for the intimate union allowed only in Matrimony. [*He bangs on the desk.*] The intimate union of the sexes is a sacred act. A duty to be done in a state of grace by a man and his wife and nobody else. So until the day you kneel at the altar with a bridal veil on your head you must never be left alone in a room with a boyfriend. Or in a field for that matter. Let the two of you go out and about with other young couples to dances and to parties and the like. But a particular word of warning about the latter. There's no doubt at all that alcoholic drinks make a party go with a swing. The danger is that after a couple of drinks a boy and a girl are more inclined to take liberties with each other. To indulge in such liberties is sinful. The girl has the special responsibility in the matter because a boy's passions are more readily aroused, God help him. Show your affection by all means. But keep to holding hands with an occasional kiss on the cheek. A Catholic boy, in his heart of hearts, will be impressed by such insistence on perfect chastity. Ask Our Blessed Lady to keep you free from the temptations of the flesh. And make no mistake about it, a passionate kiss on the lips between a boy and a girl is a serious mortal sin. [*He bangs on the desk.*] When you've the wedding ring on your finger you can fire away to your heart's content. Now has any girl any question she'd like to ask? Yes? That girl there.

MARY MOONEY: Please, Father, could you tell me what is the Sin of Sodom?

FATHER MULLARKEY: The what? Whatever put that into your head?

MARY MOONEY: It's one of the four sins crying to Heaven for vengeance, Father.

FATHER MULLARKEY: Oh yes. So it is. That's right. Well it's a very bad sin indeed. But it's nothing you need bother your head about. Sit down now. Are there any more questions? No? That'll be all then. Thank you, Mother Peter, Mother Thomas Aquinas. [*He blesses the class.*] In nomine Patris et Filii et Spiritus Sancti. Amen.

GIRLS: Good morning, Father, Thank you, Father.

SCENE TEN

[MOTHER THOMAS AQUINAS' *Office.* MARY MOONEY *is standing in front of* MOTHER THOMAS AQUINAS' *desk.*]

MOTHER THOMAS AQUINAS: What a foul, despicable creature you are. I'm thoroughly disgusted with you. Was it your own idea to ask that question, or did somebody put you up to it?

MARY MOONEY: No, Mother Thomas.

MOTHER THOMAS AQUINAS: No what? It wasn't your own idea?

MARY MOONEY: Yes, Mother Thomas. But . . .

MOTHER THOMAS AQUINAS: It was your own idea. To embarrass the poor priest in front of the entire class. May I ask why?

MARY MOONEY: I don't know, Mother Thomas.

MOTHER THOMAS AQUINAS: I'm sorry, but I don't believe you. I suggest you know full well why you chose such a question. To make yourself the centre of attraction and procure a cheap laugh at Father Mullarkey's expense. The last time you were in this office you tried to hoodwink me into believing you to be an innocent girl, immature for your years. You might like to know that I wasn't entirely convinced. And I'm now quite certain that you're not in the least bit innocent. You're an exceedingly sophisticated girl, full of knowing far beyond your years. As to the punishment, I hardly think a detention would serve any useful purpose. Instead, I am going to send you into the chapel after lunch today and every day for nine consecutive days to recite a Novena to Our Lady of Perpetual Succour. On the Saturday and Sunday you will visit your parish church. Take this. [*She takes a small booklet from her desk drawer.*] And recite the prayer on page five. 'O Mother of Perpetual

Succour behold me a miserable sinner at thy feet',
and so on. Followed by nine Hail Marys. The inten-
tion of this Novena is to ask Our Lady to alleviate
your apparent obsession with carnal knowledge
and to restore your mind and heart to childlike
innocence.

MARY MOONEY: Thank you, Mother Thomas.

MOTHER THOMAS AQUINAS: Now get out!

SCENE ELEVEN

[*A Street Corner.* MARY MCGINTY, *wearing a slightly
tarty fifties outfit, is leaning up against a wall with*
DEREK, *who has one arm around her. He puts his
other arm around her and tries to kiss her. She
turns her face away.*]

DEREK: Here, what's up with you?

MARY MCGINTY: Nothing.

[DEREK *tries to kiss her again. She turns her face
away again.*]

DEREK: What you playing at?

MARY MCGINTY: Nothing. It's dead late, Derek. I'd better be getting indoors.

DEREK: What about my goodnight?

MARY MCGINTY: Yeah. Well, goodnight then. [*She pulls away from
him and gives him a peck on the cheek.*]

DEREK: Oh yeah? You trying to drop me a hint, by any chance?
Trying to tell me something without saying nothing? Look here, darling, if I've done something
wrong I've got a right to know what it is.

MARY MCGINTY: It's nothing to do with you yourself personally.

DEREK: No? Well what is it to do with then? Eh? Come on. I
wanna know.

MARY MCGINTY: If you must know, it's to do with mortal sins.

DEREK: How's that?

MARY MCGINTY: Mortal sins. They're sins what you go to Hell for if you die with one on your soul. You know, like murder. Or eating meat on a Friday.

DEREK: Oh yeah?

MARY MCGINTY: Look, the priest came to school today to give us this big long lecture. And one of the things he said was that snogging is a mortal sin.

DEREK: Pull the other leg.

MARY MCGINTY: That's what he told us. Honestly.

DEREK: Never. You must have got it wrong. How can you go to Hell for having a snog? I mean, it's only your bloomin' cakehole after all. Wrapping it around somebody else's. Where's the harm in that for Christ's sake? You sure he wasn't talking about something a bit more on the sexy side? I mean, I know for a fact that Catholics are not allowed to . . . er . . . you know . . . until they're married. Everyone's aware of that. And myself I don't reckon it's altogether a bad idea. At least as far as girls are concerned. Myself, I wouldn't er . . . whatsname with a girl if I respected her. And I wouldn't respect a girl if she let me . . . er . . . you know. Have a bit.

MARY MCGINTY: He definitely meant snogging, Derek. I swear to you. A passionate kiss on the lips between a boy and a girl is a serious mortal sin. That's what he said. And he must know if he's the priest. D'you realise I've gone and committed hundreds of mortal sins, thanks to you.

DEREK: Oh, that's right. Put the blame on me. Ain't it marvellous, eh? I never even heard of a mortal bleedin' sin

until five fucking minutes ago. Er . . . sorry about
using that word in front of you.

MARY MCGINTY: That's all right.

DEREK: Well I mean, it's no sin for me, is it, darling?

MARY MCGINTY: No, and it's not bloomin' fair. Protestants don't
have sins, the lucky sods. I wonder where they go
when they die, though.

DEREK: They stop in the cemetery like everybody else.

MARY MCGINTY: What are you supposed to be? Church of England?

DEREK: Yeah, well, that's what I stick down if I have to fill up
a form for something or other. C of E. It don't mean
nothing, do it, except you're an ordinary English
person. It's hard luck for you, ain't it, having an Irish
Mum and Dad. You know, you don't strike me as
being one bit Irish yourself. I mean, you could easy
pass yourself off as a normal person. Funny how you
can spot a mick a mile off. No offence to your old
man or nothing. I mean, I've got nothing against
them 'part from the fact that they drink too much
and they're always picking fights among themselves. It makes me die laughing the way their hair
stands all up on end. Half of them have got that diabolical ginger hair, ain't they? And all of them have
got them big red faces. And them bleedin' great flap-
ping trousers you see them wearing down the
Kilburn High Road. You could fit half a dozen
navvies into one leg alone. I never can understand
a word they're saying. Bejasus and all that boloney.
Myself I reckon they all take religion a bit too serious.
I mean, you can understand it more with the
Italians, having the Pope stuck in the Vatican there,
keeping his eye on them. But the Irish are bleedin'
miles away. Why should they have to take orders

from the Pope? If I was you I'd be a bit suspicious of that Heaven you're so keen to get up to. It's gonna be packed out with some of the worst types of foreigners. The Irish'll be the only ones up there speaking English. The rest of them'll be Italians, Spaniards, Portuguese . . .

MARY MCGINTY: Mexicans.

DEREK: Yeah. Bolivians. Peruvians. All that mob. I can't see you fitting in somehow. No. If I was you I'd start taking it all with a pinch of salt. You don't really believe in it, do you?

MARY MCGINTY: I don't know. One minute I do, the next minute I don't.

DEREK: I know you have to make out you believe it in front of all them nuns and priests and your Mum and Dad. You don't wanna cause them no trouble. Fair enough. You can play along with it for a few more years. Then you can go your own sweet way.

MARY MCGINTY: I can't you know. Once a Catholic always a Catholic. That's the rule.

DEREK: Yeah? Tough. Oh well. Might see you around some-time.

MARY MCGINTY: Couldn't we just be mates?

DEREK: What? I've got more mates than I know what to do with. I can't have you dragging round with us up the billiard hall and down the football field. Leave off.

MARY MCGINTY: It's not that I don't wanna go out with you any more, Derek. It's just . . .

[DEREK *puts his arms around her.*]

DEREK: Come here. You can always go up to Confession on Saturday and get your soul dry cleaned. [*He kisses her. His hands go wandering and she moves them.*] Where is your soul anyway?

MARY MCGINTY: It's inside your heart.

DEREK: Don't talk rubbish.

MARY MCGINTY: I always imagine it in the heart. It could be inside your head, I suppose.

DEREK: It's not in your heart or your head. It's not in your bum neither. It don't exist.

MARY MCGINTY: There's definitely something mysterious about Confession though. It's not very nice having to tell your sins. But when you come out you feel all good and holy and all sort of excited in your head. A bit like when you've had a couple of gin and limes.

DEREK: Oooh. Touch of the old voodoo if you ask me.

MARY MCGINTY: It only lasts for about ten minutes. Then you come down to earth again and realise that just about everything you do or say or even think is a sin according to them and you just can't help committing the buggers if you're a normal human being.

DEREK: Oh well. You're just gonna have to choose between me and Jesus. [*He kisses her.*]

MARY MCGINTY: Oh Christ. Another fucking mortal sin.

DEREK: Oy! I don't wanna hear you using that sort of language.

SCENE TWELVE

[*Cuthbert's House.* MARY GALLAGHER *and* CUTHBERT, *both in school uniform, are sitting on chairs.* CUTHBERT *is holding a school copy of* Macbeth.]

MARY GALLAGHER: [*gabbling without expression*]
'Duncan is in his grave;
After life's fitful fever he sleeps well;
Treason has done his worst: nor steel, nor poison,
Malice domestic, foreign levy, nothing
Can touch him further.'

CUTHBERT: [*in a high voice*] 'Come on
Gently my lord, sleek o'er your rugged looks;
Be bright and jovial 'mong your guests tonight.'

MARY GALLAGHER: 'So shall I, love; and so, I pray be you:
Let your remembrance apply to Banquo;
Present him eminence, both with eye and tongue:
Unsafe the while, that we
Must lave our honours in these flattering streams;
And make our faces vizards to our hearts,
Disguising what they are.'

CUTHBERT: [*in a high voice*] 'You must leave this.'

MARY GALLAGHER: 'O, full of scorpions is my mind, dear wife.
Thou know'st that Banquo and his Fleance lives.'

CUTHBERT: [*in a high voice*] 'But in them nature's copy's not
eterne.'

MARY GALLAGHER: 'There's comfort yet' . . . er . . . er . . .

CUTHBERT: 'They are assailable.'

MARY GALLAGHER: 'They are assailable.' [*She looks blank.*]

CUTHBERT: 'Then be thou jocund.'

MARY GALLAGHER: Oh yes. 'Then be thou jocund; ere the bat hath
flown, His cloistered flight; ere to black Hecate's
summons.' Er . . . the . . . er . . . the something beetle
with his . . . er . . . Tut! Oh, shit! I don't know it.

CUTHBERT: Yes you do. More or less.

MARY GALLAGHER: It's got to be word perfect for Mother Peter.
Just in case she picks on me. She's such a crafty old
cow. She makes us all learn it but she'll only pounce
on one of us to test it. Whoever she happens to pick
on will have to get up and act it. In front of the whole
form. With her. She always gives herself the part of
Lady Macbeth. God, it's so embarrassing. Especially
when she starts putting on an English accent and

doing all the fancy gestures. Every time she opens her mouth a spray of spit comes flying across the classroom. We've all got to go on an outing with her next Wednesday. To see *Macbeth*. She's taking us up to the Old Vic.

CUTHBERT: Big deal.

MARY GALLAGHER: Yeah. Have you ever been there?

CUTHBERT: God, who hasn't been to the Old Vic?

MARY GALLAGHER: Lots of people haven't. My Mum and Dad for a start. Neither of them have ever set foot inside a theatre.

CUTHBERT: Peasants! [*He takes out a packet of Senior Service cigarettes, sticks one in a holder and lights it up.*]

MARY GALLAGHER: They only ever go to the pictures if a film comes round the Coliseum with a Catholic in the starring role.

CUTHBERT: Typical.

MARY GALLAGHER: They think an awful lot of Spencer Tracy. And Bing Crosby. He can do no wrong. And they both reckon the sun shines right out of Grace Kelly's arse.

CUTHBERT: How about Mario Lanza?

MARY GALLAGHER: Is he a Catholic?

CUTHBERT: He's entitled to be with a name like that.

MARY GALLAGHER: My Dad refuses to see a film if he thinks the star in it has ever been divorced. And he gets in a flaming temper if he catches sight of a picture of Lana Turner in the paper. Just because she's been married a few times. He rips the picture out of the paper and screws it up and stamps on it. [*in an Irish accent*] One husband wouldn't satisfy you, ah? Ye two-legged animal! Aaah!

CUTHBERT: I could quite fancy a session with Lana Turner.

MARY GALLAGHER: She's a bit old for you, isn't she?

CUTHBERT: Not half. I've got a definite weakness for the older woman.

MARY GALLAGHER: Oh, have you?

CUTHBERT: Yes. I have actually. [*He takes a half bottle of whisky out of his blazer pocket and has a swig.*]

MARY GALLAGHER: Can I have a drop of that?

[CUTHBERT *hands her the bottle and she takes a long swig.*]

CUTHBERT: Go easy with it. Bloody hell. That cost me eighteen and fourpence, you know.

MARY GALLAGHER: You're just stingy, you are.

CUTHBERT: No I'm not. But I only get ten bob a week off my Dad.

MARY GALLAGHER: Yeah. And the rest.

CUTHBERT: Come over here a minute.

MARY GALLAGHER: No.

CUTHBERT: Don't then.

MARY GALLAGHER: Guess who came to school today.

CUTHBERT: Cardinal Godfrey.

MARY GALLAGHER: No. Father Mullarkey actually. He was shouting his mouth off about purity.

CUTHBERT: Oh was he. Huh. I only have to hear the word purity and immediately I conjure up a picture of a fanny. And it's never any ordinary fanny. It's always a withered, shrivelled up old thing like the one the Virgin Mary's supposed to have had that they're forever saluting.

MARY GALLAGHER: I think I'd better be going.

CUTHBERT: [*offering her the whisky*] Would you like another sip? There's no such sin as impurity, you know.

MARY GALLAGHER: There is.

CUTHBERT: No there is not. A couple of thousand years ago it was taken for granted that people had uncontrollable urges. Monks used to take loose women up to their monasteries and nobody thought anything about it.

MARY GALLAGHER: Well why haven't we been taught that?

CUTHBERT: They don't want you to know, do they? Or they might not know themselves. There's an awful lot of ignorance about. I once asked my Mum if she knew how many illegitimate children Pope Alexander the Sixth had.

MARY GALLAGHER: What?

CUTHBERT: Christ, you're as bad as her. She gave me a clip round the ear. [*in an Irish accent*] 'You dirty little swine! Get out of here this minute and go and swill your mouth with soap.' She's under the impression that all the Popes were paragons of purity. Well, they bloody well weren't. They got up to all sorts of spicy things.

MARY GALLAGHER: They didn't! Did they really?

CUTHBERT: Alexander the Sixth, he was a filthy old fucker. His real name was Rodrigo Borgia. He used to knock about with various tarts. One of them owned a string of brothels. Some old bag called Vanozza. He probably picked up the syphilis off her. He was riddled with it. I found out how many bastards he had. Four. He used to have it off with his daughter. His son had the syphilis as well. I'm not making it up, you know. It's all on record in the Vatican. They've got a load of dirty documents in there all about the Popes and their concubines and bastard kids. I'm definitely going to take a trip to Rome as soon as I get the chance and have a read of them for myself.

MARY GALLAGHER: What makes you think they'd let you into the Vatican to read about stuff like that?

CUTHBERT: It happens to be open to the public. Of course they don't just let anyone in. They give out special permits. They have to, otherwise there'd be queues down there day and night.

MARY GALLAGHER: D'you think Pope Pius has girlfriends?

CUTHBERT: No. They don't do it any more. They haven't been doing it for quite a few centuries. I think it was Gregory the Seventh who put a stop to it. The cunt. Well, the way I see it is if it wasn't a sin once then it's not a sin now. You wouldn't catch me discussing my sexual habits in Confession.

MARY GALLAGHER: I don't know why you bother to go.

CUTHBERT: I'm quite prepared to confess any genuine misdeeds. Any sins against the religion itself I mean, I really believe in some of the mysteries and the majority of the doctrines. It's definitely the one true faith. And the Mass is the greatest ceremony on earth. 'Ecce Agnus Dei. Ecce qui tollit peccata mundi.' I've seriously thought about becoming a priest. It's a bloody great life. Especially if you can get into a better class of parish where they all put ten bob notes in the collection plate. I wonder if I've got a vocation. Of course, I'd have to make sure there was a bit of discreet crumpet in the background. Or I might go off my head.

MARY GALLAGHER: Cuthbert, would you know if the Sin of Sodom is supposed to be something impure according to them?

CUTHBERT: Oh yes, well that definitely is impure. Not only according to them. According to everyone. It's illegal.

MARY GALLAGHER: What exactly is it, though?

CUTHBERT: Haven't you got the slightest idea?

MARY GALLAGHER: No. That's why I'm asking you.

CUTHBERT: Well it's two blokes in one bed having it off together up their bums.

MARY GALLAGHER: Really?

CUTHBERT: Yes. I could show you some pictures if you like.

MARY GALLAGHER: Could you?

CUTHBERT: Yes. There's some going round the school at the moment. I'll let you have a look when it's my turn to borrow them. There's quite a few homosexuals at St Vincent's. I keep well out of their way. You've probably got some lessies at your school. Lesbian. That's what you call a woman homosexual. It's easy to spot a lesbian, you know. They all have very short hair and big gruff voices. They go to bed with each other and get up to all sorts of tricks with cucumbers and carrots and bananas. And candles. Most people think all nuns are rollicking lesbians. They probably are but I like to think of them keeping their vows of chastity if it kills them. There's something quite erotic about a completely celibate woman. Their natural lust gets all dammed up inside them and comes exploding out in all sorts of unexpected directions. That's why your Lady of Fatima nuns are so bad-tempered.

MARY GALLAGHER: You can say that again. They'd love to hit us if they were allowed to. But instead they find all sorts of spiteful ways to punish us. Saying sarcastic things and showing us up in front of other people. I'd sooner have corporal punishment any day.

CUTHBERT: You wouldn't say that if you'd ever had the cane off Canon O'Flynn. He's a bastard. The biggest bastard ever to come across the Irish Sea. You have to go up to his office to get it. He's always waiting for you, pacing up and down with the shillelagh in his hand and the saliva dribbling down his chin. [*in an Irish accent*] 'Are you sorry for what you've done, boy? Are you? Well you will be in a minute. Oho, you will.' Then he gets up on his chair like this. [CUTHBERT *stands on his chair and holds the copy of* Macbeth *above his head.*] 'Put out your posterior.' [MARY GALLAGHER *bends over.* CUTHBERT *jumps off the chair with a roar and hits her on the bottom with the book. She yells.* CUTHBERT *puts his arm around her.*] Oh, sorry. [*He pulls her on to his lap and puts his arms around her and kisses her.*]

MARY GALLAGHER: If I don't tell this in Confession are you sure it'll be all right to go to Holy Communion after-wards?

CUTHBERT: Of course. I've been doing that for years. Nothing's happened so it must be all right.

SCENE THIRTEEN

[*A Lavatory.* MARY GALLAGHER *and* MARY MCGINTY *are sitting on the seat with a bible between them.* MARY MOONEY *is standing up.*]

MARY MOONEY: 'And if a woman have an issue, and her issue in her flesh be blood, she shall be put apart seven days: and whosoever toucheth her shall be unclean until the even.'

MARY MCGINTY: Cor! Fancy putting that in the Bible.

MARY MOONEY: There's some better bits in Chapter Eighteen. I've underlined them in pencil. Don't let me forget to rub it out, though. My Mum would do her nut if she ever found it.

[*They turn the page.*]

MARY GALLAGHER: 'Thou shalt not uncover the nakedness of a woman and her daughter, neither shalt thou take her son's daughter or her daughter's daughter to uncover her nakedness.' Christ, those Jews must have been sex mad.

MARY McGINTY: Look at this. 'Thou shalt not lie with mankind as with womankind. It is an abomination.'

MARY GALLAGHER: That's the Sin of Sodom.

MARY McGINTY: } Is it?
MARY MOONEY:

MARY GALLAGHER: Yes. Listen to this. 'Neither shalt thou lie with any beast to defile thyself therewith.'

MARY McGINTY: A beast! Cor, blimey O'Riley.

MARY GALLAGHER: 'Neither shall any woman stand before a beast to lie down thereto. It is confusion.'

MARY McGINTY: I should say it is. Bloody hell. What sort of animals did they do it with?

MARY GALLAGHER: Whatever happened to be trotting about at the time.

MARY McGINTY: Camels.

MARY GALLAGHER: I suppose so. Horses. Pigs. Anything.

MARY MOONEY: What would it be like now if Jesus hadn't come down to put a stop to all that?

MARY McGINTY: I'd probably be going down the White Hart to-night with a monkey.

MARY GALLAGHER: You are, anyway.

MARY McGINTY: Oh, shut up.

　　　　　[MOTHER PETER *and* MOTHER BASIL *enter and go to the lavatory door.*]

MARY MOONEY: Have a look at Chapter Twenty.

　　　　　[*They turn the page.*]

MARY MCGINTY: 'And if a man shall take his sister, his father's daughter or his mother's daughter and see her nakedness and she see his nakedness . . .'

[MOTHER PETER *raps on the door.*]

MOTHER PETER: Who's in this toilet?

[*The* GIRLS *jump up and look alarmed.* MARY GALLA-GHER *puts the bible down and shushes them silently.*]

MARY GALLAGHER: [*calling out*] Me, Mother.

MOTHER PETER: Who's me?

MARY GALLAGHER: Mary Gallagher, Mother.

MOTHER PETER: Come out of there this minute, Mary Gallagher.

[MARY GALLAGHER *pulls the chain, opens the door, comes out and closes the door behind her.* MOTHER BASIL *pushes open the door and sees the other two.*]

MOTHER BASIL: Oho! We knew well there were three of you in here. Come on out of it! [*She drags them out.*]

MOTHER PETER: How dare you go into the toilet together. Big girls of your age. Were you doing anything immodest in there? Were you? Tell the truth now and shame the devil.

GIRLS: [*in unison*] No, Mother.

MOTHER BASIL: I think they were smoking. Hand over the cigarettes.

MARY GALLAGHER: We haven't been smoking, Mother.

MOTHER PETER: Well, what have you been doing in there all this time?

MARY MOONEY: We were reading the Bible, Mother.

MOTHER BASIL: You lying little toad.

MOTHER PETER: You impudent little madam, you.

[MOTHER BASIL *goes into the toilet.*]

MOTHER BASIL: There's a bible inside of this toilet, Mother Peter, believe it or not.

MOTHER PETER: Why would anyone go into the toilet to read the Bible?

> [MOTHER BASIL *comes out and hands the bible to* MOTHER PETER.]

MOTHER PETER: Whose bible is this?

> [*Pause.*]

MOTHER BASIL: Is it a Catholic bible, Mother Peter?

MOTHER PETER: Indeed it is. But I've a very strong suspicion there's more to it than meets the eye. I'm going to hand it in to Mother Thomas Aquinas and ask her to give it a thorough inspection. If the owner of this bible wants it back let her go up to Mother Thomas Aquinas' office and explain herself.

MOTHER BASIL: What are we going to do with them, Mother Peter?

MOTHER PETER: I'll deal with them later, Mother Basil. I can't imagine what kind of bad things have been going on inside that toilet. But I'll find out. I'll find out so I will.

SCENE FOURTEEN

[*The Classroom.* MOTHER PETER *is at her desk.*]

MOTHER PETER: There will be no lessons this afternoon. And no lessons again on the afternoon of the twenty-first. On that day we'll be having our little Christmas cele-bration, so bring in your cakes and snacks and your bottles of lemonade. And bring your party dresses with you to change in to. You may have the use of the gramophone, so bring along some records to dance to. Bring your hit parade records by all means.

But do not attempt to bring any Elvis Presley records into this school.

VOICES OFF: Oh no!

MOTHER PETER: Never mind your protesting. That man is a positive menace to decent young girls. I might as well tell you now that Mother Thomas Aquinas is sending out a letter to all parents to warn them about the corruption caused to innocent young minds by such a lewd and bestial artiste. Your parents have every right to go through your records, to take out the Elvis Presleys and put them into the dustbin where he belongs. There are plenty of good wholesome singers to enjoy. Joseph Locke now. He's one of the finest singers in the land. And I've heard great reports about Donald Peers. So forget about that old devil of a Presley. Now, this afternoon we're going to have a fillum show. Mother Basil is going to show us *The Barretts of Wimpole Street*. When the bell goes after lunch I want you to go straight into the Assembly Hall and take your seats for the fillum. With the exception of Mary Gallagher, Mary McGinty and Mary Mooney. These three girls will come back here to the classroom where they'll find a passage of Latin waiting to be translated into English on their desks. Mother Thomas Aquinas has asked me to make it clear that any girls seen going into the toilet together will be banned from taking their O-levels.

SCENE FIFTEEN

[*The Classroom.* MARY MCGINTY *and* MARY GALLAGHER *are singing and jiving.*]

MARY MCGINTY: Shall we show old Mooney how to jive?

[*She gets hold of* MARY MOONEY's *hand and tries to turn her round but she doesn't catch on.*]

MARY GALLAGHER: Oh, Mooney. You've got absolutely no sense
of rhythm.

MARY MOONEY: Yes I have. When I used to go Irish dancing I
was one of the best in the class.

MARY MCGINTY: Irish dancing! Sod that for a lark.

MARY GALLAGHER: Show us what you learnt.

MARY MOONEY: No fear. You'd only laugh.

MARY MCGINTY: We won't, will we?

MARY GALLAGHER: No. Come on. Just show us a couple of steps.

MARY MOONEY: No.

MARY MCGINTY: Oh go on. Be a sport.

MARY MOONEY: Oh all right.

> [MARY MOONEY *starts to do an Irish dance, with her
> arms glued to her sides and her legs leaping high
> in the air. The other two hum, 'diddly di, diddly
> di', and clap their hands.* MOTHER BASIL *comes creep-
> ing in.* MARY MCGINTY *and* MARY GALLAGHER *make
> frantic signals to* MARY MOONEY *but she is too en-
> grossed in her dance.*]

MOTHER BASIL: I see you're making a show of yourself again,
Mary Mooney. Huh. I've seen better dancing done
by a headless chicken. [*to* MARY GALLAGHER *and* MARY
MCGINTY] Get your things and go off home, you two.

> [*They go off.*]

Show me the work you were given, Mary Mooney.

> [MARY MOONEY *gives her paper to* MOTHER BASIL.]

I can't understand a word of this at all.

MARY MOONEY: It's Latin, Mother Basil.

MOTHER BASIL: Oh aren't you the sharp one, Mary Mooney.
You're so sharp you'd cut the cost of living. I'll give
you Latin, you little bitch. It isn't the Latin I'm look-

ing at at all. It's your own translation into English. Or is it Chinese or Arabic, or what? I never saw such a bad bit of writing in my life. Sit down and copy it all out again.

[*She flings the paper back at* MARY MOONEY.]

SCENE SIXTEEN

[*The Classroom.* MOTHER PETER *is at her desk.*]

MOTHER PETER: In 1917, in the thick of the first world war, a festering abscess broke out upon the face of the earth. Communism. The devil's own doctrine. When the wicked Red scoundrels took control of Russia in the 1917 Revolution this was only the start of a Communist crusade to be spread throughout the whole wide world. But in the very same year, thanks be to God, Our Blessed Lady revealed herself to three little children in Fatima. God had seen fit to intervene in the affairs of the world by sending his own Blessed Mother down to earth to start a counter-revolution.

[MARY MOONEY *comes in and stands next to* MOTHER PETER'*s desk.*]

Fatima is a village in the very centre of Portugal, about seventy miles from Lisbon. The scenery in those parts is stark and severe. I've heard tell it would put you in mind of Connemara but without the green. Mary Mooney, what time of day is this to come creeping into school?

MARY MOONEY: I'm sorry, Mother Peter, but the trolleybus came off the rails.

MOTHER PETER: Did it indeed? And why couldn't you hop off it and on to another like any normal person?

MARY MOONEY: We weren't anywhere near a bus stop, Mother Peter.

MOTHER PETER: Never mind your feeble excuses. You've missed your morning prayers. Go into the chapel now and say a few for the souls in Purgatory.

MARY MOONEY: Yes, Mother Peter.

MOTHER PETER: Now, have you got your deposit for Fatima?

MARY MOONEY: No, Mother Peter. I ...

MOTHER PETER: You haven't. Well isn't that just typical, Mary Mooney. You knew that money had to be in by today at the very latest. Isn't it just like you to be upsetting the whole schedule and making extra work for myself and Mother Thomas Aquinas. Oh, Mary Mooney, I've a good mind to exclude you from the pilgrimage altogether.

MARY MOONEY: I won't be going anyway, Mother Peter.

MOTHER PETER: Oh? And why won't you?

MARY MOONEY: My father says he can't afford it, Mother.

MOTHER PETER: Nonsense. We're getting greatly reduced rates both for the journey and the accommodation. Didn't you make that clear to your father? Of course, we know it's not a compulsory pilgrimage. Nobody is being dragged out to Fatima by the scruff of the neck. It just happens that all the other girls in this form will be going of their own free will. No doubt they'll tell you all about it when they get back. Now go to the chapel.

[MARY MOONEY *goes off.*]

On the thirteenth of each month from May to October, Our Lady appeared to Lucia dos Santos and her two little cousins Jacinta and Francisco while they were tending their sheep. There was a blinding flash and Our Lady appeared hovering over an evergreen tree. She wore a snowy white dress and veil, the dress embroidered with stars of gold, a golden cord around her neck. She had on little gold earrings and held rosary beads of sparkling white in one hand. In the other hand she held her own Immaculate Heart, bleeding and wreathed with thorns. 'I want you to do something special for me,' she told Lucia. 'I want you to ask the Pope to consecrate my Immaculate Heart to Russia. If this is done I promise that Russia will be converted. But if Russia is not converted she will spread her dreadful Communism throughout the world arousing wars and persecutions against the Church.' Our Lady promised the children that she would work a miracle and indeed she did. On the thirteenth of October seventy thousand people came to wait for the promised miracle. It was pouring with rain and the crowd made a roof of umbrellas. At noon the rain stopped and the Queen of Heaven appeared to the children. 'I am the Lady of the Rosary,' she said to Lucia. 'Let them say the rosary every day. Let them offend Our Lord no more. The war is going to end but if men do not repent then another and far more disastrous war will come.' And then she disappeared. 'Oh, look at the sun!' cried Lucia. The sun was trembling and dancing and turning like a wheel of fireworks, changing colour as it turned round and round. Then suddenly it seemed to fall towards the earth casting the colours of the rainbow on to the people and the land. The people fell into a panic thinking the world was coming to an end. But Lucia, Jacinta and Francisco were gazing in rapture up at the sky as they saw Our Lady standing to the right of the sun. She was now dressed in the blue and

white robes of Our Lady of the Rosary. To the left of
the sun St Joseph emerged from the clouds. He held
the child Jesus in his arms. Then Our Lord himself
appeared in the red robes of the Divine Redeemer
and made the Sign of the Cross three times over the
world. Beside him stood Our Lady now clad in the
purple robes of Our Lady of Sorrows. And then
finally Our Lady appeared again in the simple brown
robes of Our Lady of Carmel. The sun stopped
dancing and the crowd breathed a sigh of relief.
The world hadn't come to an end but the miracle
promised by Our Lady had come to pass. Two years
later Our Lady came to take the boy Francisco up
to Heaven. And Jacinta went up to join him the
following year. Lucia entered a convent and is still
alive and well, guarding an important secret en-
trusted to her by Our Lady. This secret will be told
to all the world as soon as Lucia receives permission
from Heaven. But until then we must all be kept in
suspense. If any of your families or friends are in
need of a miracle get them to write out their peti-
tions and we'll deliver them to Our Lady's shrine.
And while we're there we'll say a prayer for Mary
Mooney's unfortunate father. That his arms may
grow long enough to reach into his pockets. And,
by the way, even though we are going to Fatima
during the Easter holiday, Mother Thomas Aquinas
has given orders that school uniform will be worn
for the duration of the pilgrimage.

VOICES OFF: Oh no!

MOTHER PETER: Oh yes. Oh yes indeed.

SCENE SEVENTEEN

[*The Street.* MARY MOONEY, *dowdily dressed, is walking along carrying a couple of library books.* DEREK *comes swaggering along in the opposite direction. They pass each other.*]

MARY MOONEY: Hello, Derek.

DEREK: Eh? [*He stops and turns round.*] Er . . . do I know you, darling?

MARY MOONEY: Not really. But I was with Mary McGinty that day you met her along the street near our school.

DEREK: Oh yeah?

MARY MOONEY: You probably won't remember me but I'm Mary Mooney. There was another Mary with us as well that day. Mary Gallagher.

DEREK: Oh, really?

MARY MOONEY: Yes. You asked Mary McGinty if she'd meet you outside the White Hart that night. D'you remember?

DEREK: Er . . . vaguely. Bit of a long time ago, wasn't it?

MARY MOONEY: The beginning of last term. But I've got a good memory for faces.

DEREK: Oh, have you?

MARY MOONEY: Yes.

DEREK: Well, you'll have to excuse me not recognising you, darling. I mean, in them uniforms you all look like peas in a bleedin' pod. Seeing you all dressed up the way you are today, I wouldn't lump you in with none of them Lady of Fatima girls, now would I? Here, why ain't you in Fatima?

MARY MOONEY: I didn't want to go.

DEREK: Very wise, darling. Very wise. They're having a diabolical time, you know. I had a postcard Tuesday.

She's got corns coming up on her kneecaps from having to say so many prayers. They have to be in bed by nine o'clock every night. And they have to go marching about all over the place in a crocodile. [*He laughs.*] I bet you're glad you stopped in Willesden, ain't you? [*He laughs.*] I hear they carted a midget along with 'em.

MARY MOONEY: Oh, you mean Mary Finnegan in 5B. She's only as big as this. [*She holds her hand up about three feet in the air.*]

DEREK: Gonna be coming back as big as this, is she? [*He holds his hand up about six feet in the air.*]

MARY MOONEY: They're hoping she'll grow a bit bigger.

DEREK: She won't, you know. She'll be coming back as little as what she went. You wait and see.

MARY MOONEY: They won't be back for nearly another week.

DEREK: Yeah, I know. Poor sods. Here, turn your face to the side a minute. D'you know who you remind me of?

MARY MOONEY: Who?

DEREK: Rhonda Fleming.

MARY MOONEY: I don't.

DEREK: Yes you do. I see her in a film last Saturday. Yeah, you're definitely her double, you are.

MARY MOONEY: Am I?

DEREK: I'm telling you. Er . . . d'you fancy coming for a bag of chips?

MARY MOONEY: I've just had my dinner.

DEREK: Oh. Well how about a cup of tea then?

MARY MOONEY: I don't drink tea.

DEREK: Well what do you drink?

MARY MOONEY: Milk. Or water, or . . .

DEREK: What, holy water?

MARY MOONEY: Oooh, no.

DEREK: Don't look so serious, darling. They can probably do you a glass of whatever you happen to fancy round the caff.

MARY MOONEY: Well, actually, I was just on my way to the library.

DEREK: Yeah? [*He takes one of the books from under her arm.*] What's this? *The Keys of the Kingdom*, eh? Do a lot of reading do you, darling?

MARY MOONEY: There's not much else to do during the holidays.

DEREK: What's this one all about then?

MARY MOONEY: It's about a Catholic priest. Father Chisholm. He's a missionary and he goes out to China and . . .

DEREK: Sounds highly intriguing I must say. Of course, I don't go in for reading much myself. No. I'd sooner watch the old TV.

MARY MOONEY: So would I if we had one. But we haven't.

DEREK: Ain't you? Oh well, you'll have to come round my house some time and have a watch of mine. Come round this afternoon if you like.

MARY MOONEY: Oh, I don't know.

DEREK: You're more than welcome, darling. I'm not doing nothing special this afternoon. I would have gone in to work but I had such a diabolical neuralgia this morning I couldn't lift me head off of the pillow. You gonna come then?

MARY MOONEY: D'you really want me to?

DEREK: I wouldn't ask you, would I?

MARY MOONEY: All right then. I suppose I can always go to the library another day.

DEREK: Course you can. Come on then, Rhonda. Let's go and
get the bus.

SCENE EIGHTEEN

[*Derek's House.* MARY MOONEY *is sitting on the settee watching 'Bill and Ben the Flowerpot Men',
which is just ending.* DEREK *comes in carrying a
glass of orange liquid and a very large biscuit tin.*]

DEREK: Here are, mate. Glass of Tizer gone flat. That's all she
had in the cupboard.

MARY MOONEY: Oh, thanks.

[DEREK *switches off the television.*]

DEREK: Cor, bleedin' chronic, ain't it? I don't know why they
can't put nothing decent on of a daytime. Still, we've
got *The Cisco Kid* coming on a bit later, if you fancy
watching that.

MARY MOONEY: I don't know what it's all about. I've only ever
seen *Carroll Levis's Discoveries.*

DEREK: That's always good for a giggle if nothing else.

MARY MOONEY: Where's your Mum, Derek?

DEREK: Down the biscuit factory, ain't she? She does afternoons
down there. [*He offers her the tin.*] Want one?

MARY MOONEY: Oh, thanks.

[DEREK *takes off his Edwardian jacket.*]

DEREK: You can't move in this house for biscuits. She brings
'em home by the bleedin' sackful. I don't know how
she gets 'em past the gate. The old man goes round
flogging 'em to all the neighbours. [*He sits down very
close to* MARY MOONEY *and puts his arm around the back
of the settee.*] You ... er ... you going out with a
regular bloke at all?

MARY MOONEY: No.

DEREK: You must have been out with a feller or two in your time.

MARY MOONEY: Oh yes.

DEREK: Yeah, you would have done of course, a fair-looking bird like yourself. I expect you've had quite a few blokes after you, eh?

[MARY MOONEY *goes all coy.*]

DEREK: [*putting his hands up to his eyes*] Cor, that sunshine ain't half playing havoc with me neuralgia. I'm gonna have to draw them curtains. [*He gets up.*]

[*Blackout.*]

MARY MOONEY: I can't see a thing.

DEREK: No, well, I'm supposed to lie down in a darkened room whenever I get one of me attacks.

MARY MOONEY: Have you taken any aspirin?

DEREK: No. They don't do no good. Where are you? Oh, there you are. [*Pause.*] What's the matter, darling?

MARY MOONEY: I thought you were supposed to be Mary McGinty's boyfriend.

DEREK: She's in Fatima, ain't she?

MARY MOONEY: She will be coming back though.

DEREK: Look, darling, I don't wanna talk about her when I'm with you.

[*Pause.* DEREK *tuts.*]

[*whispering*] Cor, that's a choice little pair of bristol cities you got there.

MARY MOONEY: Oh no! No! No!

[*Pause. Sounds of protest from* MARY MOONEY.]

DEREK: Ssh! It's all right. We don't have to go the whole way.

Not if you don't want to. Even if we did, which I'm
not saying we would, but just supposing we did,
which we wouldn't of course, but if we did, you
wouldn't have to worry 'cos I have got something
on me, know what I mean? Give us your hand. See
what you're doing to me, darling. Cor, yeah. Now
that's better than taking an aspirin. Cor.

END OF ACT ONE

ACT TWO

SCENE ONE

[*Outside* DEREK'*s Front Door.*]

DEREK: Er ... D'you reckon you can find your own way to the bus stop, darling?

MARY MOONEY: I don't know.

DEREK: Well, what you do is, you turn left outside the gate, then you go right at the bottom of the road. Then it's the first on the right, second on the left, second on the right. Go round by the garage and through the little alleyway. That brings you out to the butcher's. Then you go left. No. I tell a lie. You go right. Walk down as far as the Coliseum, cross over the road and there's your bus stop. Right?

MARY MOONEY: I think so.

DEREK: You wouldn't mind hurrying up, would you, only I want to get the place straightened up before me Mum gets in.

[MARY MOONEY *puts her coat on.*]

Yeah. Well I might see you around some time. There's just one thing. Er ... you wouldn't go saying nothing to Mary McGinty, would you?

MARY MOONEY: No.

DEREK: No, well just make sure you don't, otherwise there could be a bit of bother and we don't want none of that. I have been known to get nasty before now, know what I mean? If you ever do bump into me any time when I'm with her, just act a little bit casual like. All right?

[MARY MOONEY *nods.*]

Right? You ready?

MARY MOONEY: I haven't got any money to get home with.

DEREK: Oh yeah. Here you are. Here's a tanner. All right? Don't forget your library books. Ta ta, mate.

[*He pats her on the bottom. She goes.*]

SCENE TWO

[*The Presbytery.* FATHER MULLARKEY *is sitting at his dinner table. He is eating a plate of sausage and mash. A plate of pudding is in front of him.* MARY MOONEY *comes in.*]

FATHER MULLARKEY: Come in and sit down, Mary Mooney.

[*She sits down at the table.*]

Miss Gavigan tells me you want to see me on a very urgent matter. Is that right?

MARY MOONEY: Yes, Father.

FATHER MULLARKEY: D'you want a sausage? [*He holds one out on a fork.*]

MARY MOONEY: No thank you, Father.

FATHER MULLARKEY: Ah, go on and have one. She's given me too many, the way she always does. [*He puts the sausage on a side plate and pushes it towards her.*] Miss Gavigan is only used to feeding great big hulks of men. She's eleven brothers back at home, not one of them under eighteen stone. Help yourself to the Lot's wife.

MARY MOONEY: The what, Father?

FATHER MULLARKEY: The salt. And put a good dollop of ketchup on it. What did you want to see me about?

MARY MOONEY: I must go to Confession, Father. Urgently.

FATHER MULLARKEY: Well, you can't go to Confession tonight. The church is all locked up and I have to get down to the off-licence.

MARY MOONEY: But I've committed a mortal sin, Father.

FATHER MULLARKEY: Ah, well, make an Act of Contrition and come up to Confession on Saturday. Could you manage a half of this old steamed pudding at all?

MARY MOONEY: No thank you, Father.

FATHER MULLARKEY: Ah, come on and help me out. I keep telling that woman, don't be giving me any more of them steamed puddings. But she doesn't take a blind bit of notice. [*He gives her half the pudding. Then he burps.*] Beg your pardon. [*He lights up a cigarette.*]

MARY MOONEY: Father, I've committed a very serious mortal sin.

FATHER MULLARKEY: Ah well, it'll surely keep till Saturday.

MARY MOONEY: I might die before then.

FATHER MULLARKEY: Not at all. A big strapping girl like yourself in the best of health.

MARY MOONEY: But I might have an accident, Father. And if I did and I died I'd be sent straight down to Hell. [*She bursts into tears.*]

FATHER MULLARKEY: Oh come on now. You can't have done anything that bad, surely.

MARY MOONEY: Oh I have, Father. I have.

FATHER MULLARKEY: Well, if it's that serious you'd better make a quick Confession now. Come over here and kneel down.

MARY MOONEY: In here, Father?

FATHER MULLARKEY: It's as good a place as any. I'll turn me back on you.

> [*She kneels down by the side of his chair. He turns away from her.*]

MARY MOONEY: Bless me Father for I have sinned. It is five days since my last Confession.

FATHER MULLARKEY: Never mind about the venial sins. Save them up for the next time. Just concentrate on the big mortal sin.

MARY MOONEY: I . . . er . . . I . . . er . . . [*Pause.*] I . . . er . . . I . . . er . . .

FATHER MULLARKEY: Was it a sin against holy purity?

MARY MOONEY: Yes, Father.

FATHER MULLARKEY: I thought as much. With another person?

MARY MOONEY: Yes, Father.

FATHER MULLARKEY: A male or a female?

MARY MOONEY: A male, Father.

FATHER MULLARKEY: A boyfriend?

MARY MOONEY: Somebody else's boyfriend.

FATHER MULLARKEY: Indeed. What did you do with him? Did you have sexual intercourse?

MARY MOONEY: No, Father. I don't think so.

FATHER MULLARKEY: You must surely know if you did or you didn't. Unless . . . Were you drunk at all?

MARY MOONEY: No, Father. But it was dark.

FATHER MULLARKEY: Did he force you to do anything?

MARY MOONEY: No, Father. But I didn't know what he was going to do until he was actually doing it.

FATHER MULLARKEY: He handled you, did he?

MARY MOONEY: Yes, Father.

FATHER MULLARKEY: How many times?

MARY MOONEY: I wasn't counting, Father.

FATHER MULLARKEY: More than once?

MARY MOONEY: Yes, Father.

FATHER MULLARKEY: And you think that's all he did?

MARY MOONEY: Yes, Father. But ... but I did something impure as well.

FATHER MULLARKEY: What?

MARY MOONEY: I don't know exactly, Father. But I think he said it was a Twentieth Century Fox.

FATHER MULLARKEY: What the devil?

MARY MOONEY: Oh, no it wasn't. It was a J. Arthur Rank.

FATHER MULLARKEY: Glory be to God. I hope you're not going to be seeing this scoundrel ever again.

MARY MOONEY: No, Father.

FATHER MULLARKEY: You know you shouldn't be left alone in a room with any man.

MARY MOONEY: Yes, Father.

FATHER MULLARKEY: You must put the whole episode right out of your mind. If it ever comes into your mind uninvited you mustn't entertain it at all.

MARY MOONEY: No, Father.

FATHER MULLARKEY: Unless, of course, you think of it with disgust instead of delight. Do you?

MARY MOONEY: Yes, Father.

FATHER MULLARKEY: That's the idea. For your penance say five Our Fathers and five Hail Marys. Now make a good Act of Contrition. Oh my God ...

MARY MOONEY: Oh my God because thou art so good I am very sorry that I have sinned against thee and by thy grace I will not sin again.

FATHER MULLARKEY: Ego te absolvo a peccatis tuis, in nomine Patris et Filii et Spiritus Sancti. Amen. [*He gets up and puts on a pair of bicycle clips.*] I must be going out now. You can stay behind and say the

penance. I'll tell Miss Gavigan not to disturb you.
Are you coming to the social on Saturday week?

MARY MOONEY: Yes, Father. I'll be coming with my mother and father.

FATHER MULLARKEY: Give my best regards to the two of them.
[*He puts his hand into his pocket and brings out a booklet.*] I wonder would you take a book of raffle tickets and see how many you can sell. We've a first prize of ten pounds. And the second is a bottle of whisky.

MARY MOONEY: Yes, Father.

FATHER MULLARKEY: Good girl. I'll leave you to it then. Goodnight.

MARY MOONEY: Goodnight, Father.

[*He goes off.*]

SCENE THREE

[*The Classroom.* MOTHER PETER *is at her desk.*]

MOTHER PETER: Now on Friday we're going to have a retreat.
The entire day will be devoted to prayer and contemplation. Father Mullarkey will give us a little talk followed by a collection for black babies in Africa. So bring in your sixpences and shillings. If the weather stays fine, please God, we plan to spend the afternoon out in the garden. You may walk up and down and say the rosary, perhaps. Or sit down and read a good book. And I don't mean any old novel. I mean the biography of a saint or some other devotional work.

[MOTHER BASIL *comes in.*]

Yes, Mother?

MOTHER BASIL: Carry on, please, Mother. I'll wait until you've finished.

MOTHER PETER: Absolute silence must be the rule for the whole day. And please do not resort to any preposterous sign language except in a case of absolute necessity. You will find the day will pass very quickly and the spiritual rewards will be very great indeed. Now, Mother Basil, can I help you at all?

MOTHER BASIL: I'm afraid I have a rather unpleasant duty to perform, Mother Peter. [*She reaches into her pocket and brings out a box of Tampax, which she holds up.*] This box of . . . of . . . things was found lying about on the floor of the downstairs cloakroom. I've been into 5B and 5C but no girl there has come forward to claim them. Indeed, they have given me their word of honour that they know nothing about them at all. And I'm inclined to believe them which means, I'm sorry to say, Mother Peter, that they must belong to a girl in 5A.

MOTHER PETER: I can't believe any girl in my form would dream of using such an immodest method of . . .

MOTHER BASIL: No self-respecting girl would abuse her body with such a contraption and that's a fact.

MOTHER PETER: Will the owner of this container please step forward and claim it. [*Long pause.*] I see. If this is to be the case then you will come to see me individually for questioning after the lesson. I'll find out whose they are. I'll find out, so I will. And whoever it is, let her shame be her only punishment.

SCENE FOUR

[*The Classroom.* FATHER MULLARKEY *is standing behind a table.* MOTHER THOMAS AQUINAS *is sitting to one side of him.*]

FATHER MULLARKEY: When Adam bit into the apple and defied

his creator he put a plague upon mankind forever after. The plague of original sin. All babies emerge from the womb infected with Adam's original sin. And there's only one way to remove this sin. By the Sacrament of Baptism. What happens to babies who die without receiving Baptism? They are prevented from entering Heaven. They must therefore go down into Hell. Not into the wretched furnace, no. But into that part of Hell known as Limbo. And what is it like in Limbo? Is it anything like Purgatory? Not a bit of it. In Purgatory the souls are punished by being heated to a degree of real discomfort. But this is only a temporary punishment. Sooner or later all the souls in Purgatory will have earned themselves a place up in Heaven. But the souls in Limbo must stay where they are for all eternity. It's a bleak old prison of a place so it is. The majority of babies in Limbo are black, yellow and brown, and if it wasn't for the wonderful work carried on by the missionaries throughout the pagan world there'd be many more babies piled up in Limbo. I'm going to send round the mission box [*He picks it up and rattles it.*] and I hope it'll be filled to the brim. Now wouldn't it be a marvellous idea if you started your very own mission box at home. Think of a little black baby and give him a name. Every week put in a percentage of your pocket money and say to yourself this is for Patrick or Joseph or Eamon so that he can be baptised and grow up to be a good Catholic. I want you to remember that Baptism is the one Sacrament that doesn't have to be administered by a priest. Anyone may baptise in a case of necessity when a priest cannot be had. If you should ever find yourself in the house of a non-Catholic friend where there's a baby who hasn't been baptised you'd do well to sprinkle water on that baby's head and say, 'I baptise thee in the name of the Father and of the Son and of the Holy Ghost. Amen.' And when you meet that child above in Heaven you can be sure he'll come up and shake you by the hand. Is it only babies that are sent to Limbo? Mostly it is. Babies and little children under the age of seven. After the age of seven a child has reached the age of reason and must decide for himself whether he wants to be good or bad. If he's wicked he'll end up in Hell like all other wicked persons. And it's the sins of the flesh that put people into Hell, make no mistake about it. The sins of the flesh. [*He bangs on the table.*] Now you may wonder about the sort of Baptism administered to our poor misguided brethren, who, though following the teachings of Christ do so within the confines of a false religion. Is the quality of their Baptism as good as our own? Indeed it is, bearing in mind that anyone can administer Baptism. We must never consider non-Catholics to be in any way inferior to ourselves. God knows it is through no fault of their own that they were born into heretical households. We must continue to pray hard for Christian unity. Pray that the heresy be removed from their hearts and that they may be guided back under the infallible umbrella of Rome. There is no other church but the Catholic Church. The Catholic Church is the one true religion. [*He bangs on the table.*] The one and only Ark of Salvation for the whole of Mankind. [*He bangs on the table again.*]

GIRLS: Good morning, Father Mullarkey. Good morning, Mother Thomas Aquinus.

SCENE FIVE

[*The Garden. The* GIRLS *are in summer uniform.*
MARY GALLAGHER, MOTHER PETER *and* MARY MOONEY
*are walking up and down in silence with rosary
beads in their hands.* MOTHER PETER'*s lips are
moving. She makes the Sign of the Cross and
goes off.* MARY GALLAGHER *does a 'V' sign after
her.*]

MARY GALLAGHER: Oh Jesus, I'm bored out of my mind.

[MARY MOONEY *puts her finger to her lips.*]

Don't tell me you're not bored.

[MARY MOONEY *shrugs her shoulders.*]

I'm sure they're trying to drive us mad. It's a well
known fact that too much silence can drive a person insane. It's all right for them. They're already
round the bend. Especially Mother Peter. If she
hadn't put herself into a convent somebody would
have locked her up in a loony bin.

MARY MOONEY: Sssh!

MARY GALLAGHER: It's all right. There's nobody about. Although
they've probably put a load of microphones into the
bushes. And they're sure to have stationed Rever-
end Mother down in the basement on a periscope.
Why the hell can't they have their idiotic retreats
in the holidays? D'you want a Smartie? [*She takes a
tube out of her pocket.*]

[MARY MOONEY *shakes her head.*]

Oh have one, will you, for Christ's sake. We're not
supposed to be fasting, you know. Hold out your
hand. [*She pours some Smarties into* MARY MOONEY'*s
reluctant hand.*] Are you keeping quiet just to annoy
me, by any chance?

[MARY MOONEY *shakes her head.*]

I suppose you're scared of getting caught.

MARY MOONEY: No I'm not.

MARY GALLAGHER: You are.

MARY MOONEY: I'm not.

MARY GALLAGHER: Well, what are you being so holy for? Come to think of it, though, you always have been a bit that way inclined.

MARY MOONEY: I have not. I'm no more holy than you are.

MARY GALLAGHER: Not much. I doubt if you've ever committed a genuine mortal sin in all your life.

MARY MOONEY: Oh yes I have. I've definitely committed one.

MARY GALLAGHER: Oooh, one. That's a lot isn't it.

MARY MOONEY: Why, how many have you committed?

MARY GALLAGHER: Millions.

MARY MOONEY: Have you really?

MARY GALLAGHER: Yes. You know that box of Tampax?

MARY MOONEY: Yes.

MARY GALLAGHER: They were mine.

MARY MOONEY: They weren't!

MARY GALLAGHER: They were, you know.

MARY MOONEY: Why didn't you go up and claim them?

MARY GALLAGHER: You must be joking. She didn't suspect me for a minute.

MARY MOONEY: Who got the blame in the end?

MARY GALLAGHER: Maria Zajaczkowski.

MARY MOONEY: That wasn't very fair.

MARY GALLAGHER: She's not bothered. They could just as easily have been hers. She went red when Mother Peter

cross-examined her. Did you know she's going out
with a really old man?

MARY MOONEY: No.

MARY GALLAGHER: Yes. He must be at least twenty-five. Nearly
everybody in our form has got a bloke. It's time you
got yourself one, isn't it?

MARY MOONEY: You think I've never been out with a bloke, don't
you?

MARY GALLAGHER: Well you haven't, have you?

MARY MOONEY: Oh yes I have, if you want to know.

MARY GALLAGHER: Oh yes? Since when?

MARY MOONEY: Since just after Easter, actually.

MARY GALLAGHER: How come you've kept so quiet about it,
then?

MARY MOONEY: If I told you something really confidential would
you promise to keep it a secret?

MARY GALLAGHER: Yes, of course.

MARY MOONEY: Would you swear to God never to tell a soul?

MARY GALLAGHER: Yes. You can trust me.

MARY MOONEY: Cross your heart and hope to die.

MARY GALLAGHER: All right.

MARY MOONEY: You know when you were in Fatima?

MARY GALLAGHER: Yes.

MARY MOONEY: Well, I met a bloke in the street and he asked
me to go to his house with him, so I did.

MARY GALLAGHER: What, you let a bloke pick you up just like
that? And you didn't even know who he was?

MARY MOONEY: No. I mean yes. I did know who he was. That's
just the trouble. You know who he is too.

MARY GALLAGHER: Who?

MARY MOONEY: Promise you won't tell anyone in all the world. Especially not Mary McGinty.

MARY GALLAGHER: Why not her?

MARY MOONEY: Well, see, this bloke . . . It was her boyfriend Derek.

MARY GALLAGHER: Cor! No!

MARY MOONEY: Yes.

MARY GALLAGHER: Are you sure you're not making it up? I can't imagine you and him together.

MARY MOONEY: Well we were.

MARY GALLAGHER: Christ. She'd go berserk if she ever knew.

MARY MOONEY: You won't tell her will you? Please.

MARY GALLAGHER: I wouldn't dare. Did he ask to see you again?

MARY MOONEY: I wouldn't want to see him again, not as long as I live. He's horrible.

MARY GALLAGHER: Is he? How come Mary McGinty's so mad about him then?

MARY MOONEY: He was nice at first. But then he turned nasty. Well not exactly nasty but rude. Do all blokes try to do rude things to girls?

MARY GALLAGHER: The majority of them, yes, if they get the chance.

MARY MOONEY: Has Cuthbert ever tried to be impure?

MARY GALLAGHER: He never thinks about anything else.

MARY MOONEY: But he's a Catholic.

MARY GALLAGHER: Yes. Terrible, isn't it.

MARY MOONEY: You've been going out with Cuthbert for a long time, haven't you?

MARY GALLAGHER: What about it?

MARY MOONEY: Is that why you've committed so many mortal sins? Because he makes you?

MARY GALLAGHER: He doesn't make me. What a thing to say. It's the devil who makes you commit sins.

MARY MOONEY: That Derek must be possessed by the devil.

MARY GALLAGHER: Why? What did he do? Oh dear, you haven't lost your priceless virginity, have you?

MARY MOONEY: No. No . . . but . . .

MARY GALLAGHER: What?

MARY MOONEY: I couldn't possibly tell you.

MARY GALLAGHER: I've probably heard it all before.

MARY MOONEY: I couldn't possibly say what he did. But I've got it written down in my diary. [*She takes a book out of her pocket.*] I have to keep it with me all the time in case anyone should ever find it. My Mum'd swing for me if she saw it. You can have a look at it if you like.

MARY GALLAGHER: [*reading the diary*] Cor, fancy letting a bloke do that to you the first time you ever go out with him.

MARY MOONEY: I didn't want him to. But he was a lot stronger than me. He's not like a boy, that Derek. He's a proper big man, you know.

MARY GALLAGHER: They will usually stop if you tell them to.

MARY MOONEY: I did. But he said we all know 'no' means 'yes'. That doesn't make any sense though, does it?

MARY GALLAGHER: It means you liked what he was doing but you didn't want to admit it.

MARY MOONEY: I did not like it.

MARY GALLAGHER: Didn't you? You must be abnormal then.

MARY MOONEY: I'm not.

MARY GALLAGHER: You must be. Everybody else likes it.

MARY MOONEY: Well it wasn't all that bad, I suppose.

MARY GALLAGHER: You want to find a bloke of your own. It's not the done thing to go round borrowing other people's.

MARY MOONEY: Oh, shut your rotten face. And give me back my diary.

> [*She snatches the diary and goes marching off.* MARY MCGINTY *is sitting on a bench with a book.* MARY GALLAGHER *goes up and sits next to her.*]

MARY MCGINTY: How much longer have we got?

MARY GALLAGHER: Another couple of hours.

MARY MCGINTY: Oh, Christ. I can't stand it. Have you finished your book?

MARY GALLAGHER: No. I haven't read a word of it. I've been talking to Mary Mooney.

MARY MCGINTY: I bet she was keeping her mouth well shut.

MARY GALLAGHER: Not exactly, no. Actually there's more to that girl than you might think.

MARY MCGINTY: How d'you mean?

MARY GALLAGHER: She's a bit of a dark horse if you did but know. I've found out she's got a dead sly streak in her.

MARY MCGINTY: Really?

MARY GALLAGHER: I know it for a fact. I can't very well tell you what I've found out about her, though. I would tell you only it's something to do with you and you wouldn't like it if you knew.

MARY MCGINTY: You might as well tell me. Go on.

MARY GALLAGHER: You'll only be furious, I warn you. It's something that happened while we were away in Fatima.

MARY MCGINTY: What? Come on.

MARY GALLAGHER: Well . . . she met a bloke in the street and went back to his house with him.

MARY MCGINTY: What's that got to do with me?

MARY GALLAGHER: It was your Derek. The bloke.

MARY MCGINTY: My Derek?

MARY GALLAGHER: Yes.

MARY MCGINTY: He wouldn't look at Mary Mooney.

MARY GALLAGHER: He might not look at her. But he definitely went and touched her.

MARY MCGINTY: Eh? Is that what she told you?

MARY GALLAGHER: She's got it all written down in her diary. All the sordid details.

MARY MCGINTY: What, you mean you've read it?

MARY GALLAGHER: Yes.

MARY MCGINTY: [*jumping up*] I'll bleedin' kill her. Little slag. And him. Filthy dirty sod.

> [*She goes marching off.* MOTHER BASIL *and* MARY MOONEY *enter followed by* MARY MCGINTY. MARY MCGINTY *goes over to* MARY MOONEY.]

MARY MCGINTY: I wanna talk to you.

MARY MOONEY: What about?

MARY MCGINTY: You know bleedin' well what about.

MARY MOONEY: I suppose you've been gossiping with your friend Mary Gallagher.

MARY MCGINTY: Haven't I just.

MARY MOONEY: She promised me she wouldn't tell you.

MARY MCGINTY: You should know better than to open your big fat mouth, shouldn't you, you little scrubber. Making out you're so frigging holy. Why can't you get a bloke of your own?

MARY MOONEY: Look, I'm sorry. I didn't mean . . . Oh, I wish I'd never.

MARY MCGINTY: You gonna let me have a look at that dirty little diary of yours?

MARY MOONEY: No.

MARY MCGINTY: Why not? You let Mary Gallagher see it. You can just let me see it and all. It's my bleedin' bloke you've been scribbling about. Where is it?

> [*She tries to take the diary out of* MARY MOONEY'*s pocket.* MARY MOONEY *struggles but* MARY MCGINTY *gets hold of it.*]

MARY MOONEY: Give it back. You mustn't read it. Please give it back to me. Please.

> [MOTHER BASIL *comes marching along.* MARY MCGINTY *drops the diary and goes off.* MOTHER BASIL *comes up to* MARY MOONEY *and shakes her fist at her. They both bend down to pick up the diary and their heads collide.* MOTHER BASIL *gives* MARY MOONEY *a punch. She falls down.* MOTHER BASIL *starts kicking her.* MOTHER BASIL *goes marching off in a temper with the diary but turns round and comes back again to deliver one final kick.*]

SCENE SIX

> [*Derek's House.* MARY MCGINTY *is sitting on the settee.* DEREK *is pacing up and down, chain-smoking.*]

DEREK: Look, I've told you a hundred times, she didn't mean nothing. And I didn't do nothing neither. Nothing much anyway. I mean, be fair. She come up and spoke to me in the street. I never knew her from Old Mother Hubbard, did I? You know how it is when I get me attacks of neuralgia. Me eyesight gets affected, don't it. I couldn't make out what she looked like in the street. She could have been a really beau-

tiful bird for all I knew. When I got her inside the
house and see what she really looked like I had to
draw the curtains double quick. I should have
known that was asking for trouble, though, 'cos
once you're in the dark with somebody it might just
as well be anybody, you know how it is. Oh, no, you
don't, of course. Well I'm only human, know what
I mean? Not like you. No. You're about as warm as
a Lyons choc ice you are, darling. It's about bleedin'
time you faced up to the fact that I've been impair-
ing me capabilities for the sake of respecting you.
It's a wonder I ain't done myself some sort of a per-
manent mischief Not that I get any credit for it, oh
no. It's all been a bleedin' waste of time. It's quite
obvious you don't wanna go out with me no more.

MARY MCGINTY: I didn't say that.

DEREK: You don't have to say it. I'm going by the way you're
acting towards me.

MARY MCGINTY: Did she sit on this?

DEREK: I don't remember.

MARY MCGINTY: Yes you do. Which side did she sit on?

DEREK: The other side.

MARY MCGINTY: You sure?

DEREK: What difference does it make? Me Mum's been over it
with the Hoover tons of times since then. She's got
one of them attachments that gets right into all the
corners.

MARY MCGINTY: I'm just wondering how many other birds
you've been out with behind my back while you're
supposed to have been going out with me.

DEREK: None.

MARY MCGINTY: I don't believe you. Anyway, I've heard otherwise.

DEREK: Who from?

MARY MCGINTY: Somebody who's seen you about.

DEREK: Well . . . they was only a couple of little tarts. I mean, I don't go looking for it, darling. But if it happens to come my way . . . I can't very well help myself, can I? And who in this world would blame me the way you behave towards me. You know my old Nan was half Italian, don't you?

MARY MCGINTY: Never mind your Nan. How many girls did you say you'd been out with?

DEREK: I told you. A couple.

MARY MCGINTY: How many's a couple?

DEREK: I don't know. Five or six.

MARY MCGINTY: What were their names?

DEREK: Gloria. Joyce. I don't know. I wasn't bothered about their names. Here, what's all this interrogation in aid of? I don't ask you no questions, do I? For all I know you could have been running about with all sorts of greasy foreigners out in Fatima.

MARY MCGINTY: Oh yeah? Some chance of that with the nuns breathing down our necks day and night.

DEREK: That's what you tell me.

MARY MCGINTY: I did not go out with anyone in Fatima or anywhere else. But I bleedin' well would in the future.

DEREK: Would you?

MARY MCGINTY: You bet your life I would.

DEREK: Oh well. Please yourself

MARY MCGINTY: Don't worry. I will.

[*Pause.*]

DEREK: Er . . . you wouldn't . . . er . . . No. It's just a thought. No. I mean . . . You can laugh if you like but how

about . . . no. How about . . . er . . . d'you . . . er
. . . d'you . . . d'you . . . er . . . d'you fancy getting engaged?

MARY MCGINTY: What?

DEREK: You heard.

MARY MCGINTY: Are you in love with me?

DEREK: Eh ? [*He takes out his comb and combs his hair.*]

MARY MCGINTY: Yes or no.

DEREK: [*doing a terrible impersonation of Elvis Presley singing and gyrating*]
'Well bless my soul what's wrong with me
I'm shaking like a bear up in a honey tree
My friends say I'm acting just as wild as a bug
I'm in love, Ooh, I'm all shook up.
Uh huh huh, uh huh, yeah, yeah, yeah.'

MARY MCGINTY: You don't have to take the piss.

DEREK: I wasn't in actual fact. I meant what I was singing.

MARY MCGINTY: Oh. Are you offering to buy me a ring by any chance?

DEREK: Yeah. Don't expect nothing too flash, though. I ain't no millionaire.

MARY MCGINTY: Does that mean you'd actually want to get married some time?

DEREK: I probably would in a couple of years.

MARY MCGINTY: Before or after you do your National Service?

DEREK: There won't be none of that, darling. No. Not with this neuralgia.

MARY MCGINTY: I hope you get away with it.

DEREK: I will.

MARY MCGINTY: Why d'you want to marry me, Derek?

DEREK: Be a bit of a laugh, wouldn't it?

MARY MCGINTY: Oh, thanks very much.

DEREK: Well ... I just happen to think you're one of the best-looking birds I've seen knocking about Willesden for a long time. And I wouldn't mind kipping down in the same bed as you every night. If it was all right with you.

MARY MCGINTY: I wouldn't mind getting engaged to you.

DEREK: Oh. I didn't think you'd want to somehow.

MARY MCGINTY: Don't you want me to, then?

DEREK: Course I do, darling. I wouldn't have asked you, would I?

MARY MCGINTY: Well, I've said I would.

DEREK: Yeah, well that's all right then, ain't it.

[*Long pause.*]

MARY MCGINTY: How would you feel about changing your religion, though?

DEREK: Do what? Leave off, mate.

MARY MCGINTY: But if you really want to marry me, Derek, you'll have to marry me in a Catholic church.

DEREK: Oh no! No chance. No. That's definitely out, darling. I was thinking more along the lines of a register office myself.

MARY MCGINTY: If I got married in a register office I'd be living in sin in the eyes of the Catholic Church.

DEREK: All right, so change over to the Church of England.

MARY MCGINTY: Look, Derek, I've told you before. It's once a Catholic always a Catholic and that's all there is to it. We're not even allowed to set foot inside the door of a Protestant church without getting permission off of a Bishop.

DEREK: No, but you expect people to come crawling into your churches whenever it suits you, oh yes.

MARY MCGINTY: That's only because the Catholic Church is the real Christian church. In fact it's the only proper religion in the world. The others are all phoney.

DEREK: Is that right? Who said so, eh? Who laid that one down?

MARY MCGINTY: Jesus.

DEREK: He's got some cheek, ain't he? The only religion, eh? That's a downright diabolical insult to all the people in this country who go toddling off to the Church of England of a Sunday morning. And that includes my Aunt Ada and my Uncle Ernie. And my cousin Freda. Yeah, and the Queen. They're all in the wrong, are they? And the Irish are in the right? Yeah? Rhubarb. Fucking rhubarb, darling. And I don't intend to apologise for saying that word in front of you. And what about all the other people in the world, eh? The Hindus and the Mohammedans and the Four by Twos. They don't count for nothing with Jesus, do they? Oh no. Jesus only cares about the Irish. Anybody else is just a load of bleedin' riff-raff. He come all the way down to Earth, did he, all the way to Nazareth for the benefit of the bleedin' Irish? Yeah. Very likely. Why didn't he go straight to Dublin, eh? Why not? He could have had a great time changing all the water into Guinness and dancing about to ceilidh bands.

MARY MCGINTY: Oh, shut up, Derek. I can't help the way I was brought up. I've got to think of my Mum and Dad. How would they feel if I went and got married out of the Church?

DEREK: And what about my Mum and Dad? Of course I realise they're only a pair of little old Protestants. It don't matter about them having to get stunk out with incense and having to listen to a load of hocus fucking pocus. No. Don't worry about them.

MARY MCGINTY: Oh, sod you, Derek.

DEREK: Sod you and all, mate.

[MARY MCGINTY *gets up and grabs her coat.*]

MARY MCGINTY: I'm going home.

DEREK: Go on then.

MARY MCGINTY: I hope they put you in the bleedin' army and shave off all your hair.

DEREK: Thanks.

[MARY MCGINTY *moves off but* DEREK *goes after her and gets hold of her.*]

Come here, you silly cow. Look, why can't we just leave it at getting engaged and save all the rest of the rubbish for later on?

MARY MCGINTY: No. It's something that has to be settled now.

DEREK: Well I ain't changing into no Catholic, darling. I just ain't got it in me.

MARY MCGINTY: You don't have to change. But I have to get married in a Catholic church.

[DEREK *puts his arms around her.*]

DEREK: What if I said I might. They wouldn't expect nothing of me, would they?

MARY MCGINTY: You'd have to sign a document to promise you'd bring all your children up as Catholics.

DEREK: All me what? Here, hang about. You're being a little bit previous, ain't you? It just so happens I ain't all that struck on little nippers with nappies full of squashed up turds.

MARY MCGINTY: But we'd have to have children if we got married.

DEREK: Yeah. One maybe. Or possibly two. But I draw the line at fucking football teams. Er ... sorry about using that word. But I've seen enough of them Irish women down in Kilburn. Two in the pram. Three more hanging on to the handle. And half a dozen more waiting outside the boozer for the Daddy to come rolling out. No. You have your Catholic wedding, mate, and I'll have me packet of three. All right?

SCENE SEVEN

[*Cuthbert's House.* CUTHBERT *is lying on the settee. He is wearing a silk dressing gown, school socks and carpet slippers.* MARY GALLAGHER *is sitting on the floor with a bottle of whisky by the side of her. They each have a glass of whisky and their speech is slightly slurred.* CUTHBERT *is smoking a Senior Service cigarette in a holder.*]

CUTHBERT: [*holding out his glass*] Pass the bottle up, would you? It's time I had a refill.

MARY GALLAGHER: You'll be lucky. It's nearly all gone.

[*She shows him the empty bottle.*]

CUTHBERT: We haven't drunk all that, have we? Fucking hell. I was hoping to top it up with water and put it back in the cupboard.

MARY GALLAGHER: You wouldn't have got away with that.

CUTHBERT: I've done it before enough times. He drinks so much himself he doesn't know what he's drinking half the time. And he'll be completely out of his mind by the time he comes rolling back from the County Mayo.

MARY GALLAGHER: And your Mum'll still be crying.

CUTHBERT: Yeah. Christ knows what for. She's been waiting for the old faggot to snuff it for the past twenty years.

MARY GALLAGHER: Did you know your Granny very well?

CUTHBERT: I only met her a couple of times when I was a little kid. I remember she had a beard. And bunions. Two of the biggest bunions you ever saw in your life, trying to force their way out of the side of each boot. Apparently she never used to wear any drawers. Whenever she wanted to go for a piddle she'd just walk out to the cowshed, stand with her legs apart and let it flow. I can well believe it. They never had any toilets when I was taken over there as a kid. You had to sit on a smelly old bucket and wipe your arse with a handful of shamrock. Or whatever it is that grows over there. I'm bleedin' glad I didn't have to go this time. Although I hear they have got toilets now.

MARY GALLAGHER: My Mum and Dad would never have trusted me on my own for a whole week.

CUTHBERT: They didn't have much choice. I couldn't very well leave my exams.

MARY GALLAGHER: One of them would have stayed behind in our house. They're a hell of a lot more suspicious than yours.

CUTHBERT: That's because you're a girl.

MARY GALLAGHER: Yeah. You're probably right. I only hope they don't go checking up to see if I'm at Mary McGinty's tonight.

CUTHBERT: Oh, sod 'em. Could you do me a big favour? See if there's anything else to drink in the cupboard.

[MARY GALLAGHER *gets up and goes to the cupboard and brings out a load of bottles.*]

MARY GALLAGHER: There's no more whisky.

CUTHBERT: I know, worse luck.

MARY GALLAGHER: There's one bottle of Guinness. And apart from that it's mostly just dregs.

CUTHBERT: You might as well get it all out and we'll finish it up.

MARY GALLAGHER: Are you sure you won't get into trouble?

CUTHBERT: I'll think about that when the time comes. We'll have half the Guinness each and we can top it up with the various dregs.

[MARY GALLAGHER *pours out the drinks.*]

I'll have to go and buy another bottle of whisky though. She's left me forty-five bob for food and stuff. A bottle of whisky is what? Thirty-six bob. Christ, I won't have much left over, will I?

MARY GALLAGHER: You could always come round to our house for dinner one night.

CUTHBERT: I wouldn't mind. But your Mum doesn't like me very much, does she?

MARY GALLAGHER: It's not you she doesn't like as much as your language.

CUTHBERT: Eh?

MARY GALLAGHER: She says it's a bit too ripe for a boy of your age.

CUTHBERT: What does she mean, ripe?

MARY GALLAGHER: She said she heard you swearing in our front room.

CUTHBERT: She shouldn't be fucking listening, should she?

MARY GALLAGHER: You might know they'd listen when you're in there with me. And they look through the key-hole. It's only to be expected.

CUTHBERT: Wait till she hears I'm going to be a priest.

MARY GALLAGHER: You're not going to be any priest.

CUTHBERT: Oh yes I am. I went into Canon O'Flynn the other day and told him I'd got a vocation.

MARY GALLAGHER: What did he say to that?

CUTHBERT: He said he wasn't at all surprised. He'd guessed it all along.

MARY GALLAGHER: I bet you didn't tell him your views on celibacy.

CUTHBERT: There's no reason why I should. He hasn't told me his.

MARY GALLAGHER: They're bound to be slightly more conventional than yours. How could you possibly be a priest?

CUTHBERT: I can. And I will. There's nothing else I want to do. [*He sings.*] 'Credo in unum Deum, Patrem omnipotentem, factorem caeli et terrae, visibilium omnium, et invisibilium. Et in unum Dominum'. . .

MARY GALLAGHER: Oh, shut up, will you. I hear enough of that every Sunday.

CUTHBERT: Well I don't. I never get tired of the Mass.

MARY GALLAGHER: Mother Peter says they'll be saying it in English before another decade is out.

CUTHBERT: What? They'd better not or I'll be kicking up the most appalling stink. It'd be no better than the Church of England. I'd have to do a defection to the Russian Orthodox. Or the Greek. No, they couldn't possibly change it. It's only a rumour.

MARY GALLAGHER: It might not be such a bad idea. At least ordinary people would be able to understand it.

CUTHBERT: Huh. They can understand the Stations of the Cross and look how boring they are.

MARY GALLAGHER: You'd have to say them if you become a priest.

CUTHBERT: Only during Lent. I could always speed them up a bit or miss a couple out. Nobody'd notice. I can't expect to enjoy every duty I'd have to perform.

MARY GALLAGHER: How do you feel about hearing Confessions?

CUTHBERT: I'd never ask anyone: 'How many times?' [*He yawns.*] I think it's time for bed.

MARY GALLAGHER: It's not. It's only half past eight.

CUTHBERT: You'd better go out by the back door in the morning. Just to be on the safe side. In case one of the neighbours happens to see you.

MARY GALLAGHER: I'll go straight round to Mary McGinty's and go to Mass with her.

CUTHBERT: Are you any good at washing?

MARY GALLAGHER: What d'you mean?

CUTHBERT: Well, you know my bed's only a little one. It's the same one I've had since I was six. We could go in my Mum and Dad's only I'd have to put some clean sheets on afterwards. There's one or two shirts I'd like washing as well. And some socks.

MARY GALLAGHER: Oh. All right.

CUTHBERT: Shall we go?

MARY GALLAGHER: Not yet. You will still respect me tomorrow, won't you Cuthbert?

CUTHBERT: Yes, of course.

MARY GALLAGHER: D'you promise?

CUTHBERT: Yes. Come on. I've got to be serving on the altar at seven o'clock Mass tomorrow morning.

SCENE EIGHT

[*A Side Room.* MR EMANUELLI *is sitting on a chair.*
MARY MOONEY *is standing in front of him, singing.*
He is conducting her with one of his walking sticks.
She is wearing Nanki-Poo's Japanese costume with
a false bald head and a pigtail.]

MARY MOONEY: [*singing*]
'And if you call for a song of the sea
We'll heave the capstan round
With a yeo-heave ho, for the wind is free
Her anchor's a-trip and her helm's a-lee
Hurrah for the homeward bound.'

MR EMANUELLI: [*singing*]
'Yeo-ho, heave ho.
Hurrah for the homeward bound.'

MARY MOONEY: 'To lay aloft in a howling breeze
May tickle a landsman's taste
But the happiest hour a sailor sees
Is when he's down at an inland town
With his Nancy on his knees, yeo-ho
And his arm around her waist.'

MR EMANUELLI: 'Then man the capstan off we go
As the fiddler swings us round
With a yeo-heave ho and a rum below
Hurrah for the homeward bound
With a yeo-heave ho
And a rum below
Yeo-ho, heave ho,
Yeo-ho, heave ho, heave ho, heave ho, yeo-ho.'
[*He hums.*] La, la, la, la . . .

MARY MOONEY: 'A wandering minstrel I
A thing of shreds and patches
Of ballads, songs and snatches

And dreamy lullaby
And dreamy lul-la, lul-la-by
Lul-la-by.'

MR EMANUELLI: It will have to do. The vibrato is all up the creek
but it's the best we can manage for the moment. But
please, please do not let me see you slinking on to
the stage and apologising to the audience for your
presence.

MARY MOONEY: No, Sir.

MR EMANUELLI: You must learn to stand up for yourself or you'll
find yourself trampled right into the ruddy ground.
It will be better for you when you go away from this
dump of a sanctimonious institution. You will go
and study music. Learn to control your respiration,
sing in Italian and enlighten your ear. I will help
you. Do you have a gramophone at home?

MARY MOONEY: Oh yes, Sir.

MR EMANUELLI: What do you listen to on it?

MARY MOONEY: Irish records mostly, Sir.

MR EMANUELLI: Huh. What ruddy use is that to you? Eh? No.
You will come in the holidays to my house and you
will hear Mozart and Puccini. Come the first Wednesday afternoon at three o'clock. Do you know how
to get to Hendon Central?

MARY MOONEY: Yes, Sir. But . . .

MR EMANUELLI: [*getting out pen and paper*] Here is my address.
Bang hard on the window and I will throw you out
the key. It will be good to have a visitor. Nobody
comes to see me any more. I can't say I blame them.
I wouldn't come to see me myself. Why such a face?
Eh? Do you think I am putting you into a catapult
and firing you off into a career you don't want really?

MARY MOONEY: No, Sir.

MR EMANUELLI: Well, I cannot guess what is in your mind. Does this leg of mine offend you?

MARY MOONEY: No, Sir.

MR EMANUELLI: I don't see why it shouldn't when it certainly offends me.

MARY MOONEY: I've got used to it, Sir.

MR EMANUELLI: Well, I tell you something. I can't ever get used to it. What kind of God is he up there to send me such an affliction when I haven't done nothing to him?

MARY MOONEY: He often sends suffering to good people, Sir. It's really a privilege in disguise.

MR EMANUELLI: What kind of talk is that, eh? It's not the talk of a young girl. It's the talk of a blasted nun. I loathe and detest nuns. I despise every one of them in this building. They should be tied up with string, laid out in a line and raped by the local police. Take no notice. I am being cantankerous. Some days I feel so cantankerous I could take a machine gun into the streets and shoot down the whole population of Hendon Central. I don't know why. I would never have come to this convent if I could have found a little work somewhere else.

MARY MOONEY: I'll pray for your leg to get better, Sir.

MR EMANUELLI: Thank you very much but don't bother. I've tried it myself. Candle after candle burning uselessly in front of a statue of St Francis of Assisi. A million Hail Marys wafting up into the empty atmosphere. Even a journey to Lourdes, wouldn't you know. Never in all my life did I experience such humiliation. Seeing myself lumped in among so many wretched unfortunates. I came hobbling home and decided it was time for Maximilian Emanuelli to disappear from the face of the earth. I was going to go by way of the gas oven. With one hundred codeine tablets inside my belly. Every day I had a dress rehearsal. There never could be an actual performance. Of course there couldn't. How could there be? No matter how unbearable his precious life on earth, if a Catholic dares to put an end to it himself there'll be a far worse existence waiting on the other side. Huh. I don't believe a word of it and yet I know it's true. I will be shouting for the priest to come running with the Sacrament of Extreme Unction as soon as I see the Angel of Death approaching. I must be saved from the fires of Hell even though I know I would find in Hell all the people with whom I have anything in common. Especially Rudolph, who always said he would happily burn in Hell, the swine. For eighteen years he and I were together, all the time laughing, mostly at other people. It's a good thing he went on before me. He never would have stood for this leg. You are too young and green to comprehend such things but I hope in your life one day there will be a Rudolph. But you won't find him in Willesden or Harlesden or Neasden or Acton or Dollis Hill. You must travel all over the world and meet lots of fascinating people. And you must learn to be fascinating yourself. You are not a good-looking girl but you can cheat. With the help of something colourful out of a bottle you can soon enrich the miserliness of nature. [*He sings.*] 'Paint the pretty face, dye the coral lip. Emphasise the grace of her ladyship.' [*He gets up.*] Now I have to go and inspect the orchestra. You will show me a good performance, yes?

MARY MOONEY: Yes, Sir.

MR EMANUELLI: [*taking a medal and chain out of his pocket*] I have something nice for you. Here. It was once given to me and now I give it to you with my very best wishes.

MARY MOONEY: Thank you, Sir. What is it?

MR EMANUELLI: The eye of Horus. [*He puts it round her neck.*] Horus was an Egyptian god who roamed the earth a long long time ago. He was highly esteemed by the pagans. Let him bring you a little bit of luck.

> [MR EMANUELLI *pats* MARY MOONEY *on the shoulder and goes off.* MARY MOONEY *wrenches the chain from her neck and hurls it across the room.*]

SCENE NINE

[MOTHER THOMAS AQUINAS' *Office.* MOTHER THOMAS AQUINAS *is at her desk.* MARY GALLAGHER *is sitting in front of her.*]

MOTHER THOMAS AQUINAS: Well, congratulations, Mary Gallagher.

MARY GALLAGHER: Thank you, Mother Thomas.

MOTHER THOMAS AQUINAS: You've done extremely well and we're all very pleased with you indeed. You'll go into the academic sixth form next year and we'll work towards getting you a place at university. Have you any idea at all about what you might like to take up as a career?

MARY GALLAGHER: I've thought about working in a laboratory, Mother. And I've thought about teaching Physics and Chemistry.

MOTHER THOMAS AQUINAS: You could do a lot worse than teach, my dear. Do you know, I really miss the teaching myself, after so many years of it. I never imagined I'd be sitting behind a desk all day with so much responsibility on my shoulders. But God knows best of course. It isn't for me to question his methods. Ah well. You'll find things very different in the academic sixth. Would you like to be a prefect?

MARY GALLAGHER: I'm not sure, Mother.

MOTHER THOMAS AQUINAS: Well, I'd like you to become a prefect and help me keep the younger girls on their toes. There's just one thing that worries me slightly about you, my dear, and that's your rather strange choice of companions. When you do go up to the sixth form you will be mixing with a different set of girls. You can look forward to a most satisfactory and perhaps even a brilliant future with the help of God. All the best to you now and have a very enjoyable holiday.

MARY GALLAGHER: Yes, Mother Thomas. Thank you, Mother Thomas.

> [MARY GALLAGHER *gets up and goes off.* MARY MCGINTY *comes in and stands in front of* MOTHER THOMAS AQUINAS.]

MOTHER THOMAS AQUINAS: Well now, Mary McGinty, I'm sorry to have to say, your examination results were very disappointing indeed. Do you get nervous during exams at all?

MARY MCGINTY: Yes, Mother. A bit.

MOTHER THOMAS AQUINAS: Your work has always been up to standard if not particularly original. It's a shame to see you ending up with such a poor record. Have you any thoughts on a career at all?

MARY MCGINTY: No, Mother.

MOTHER THOMAS AQUINAS: Well, I'd like you to go into the secretarial sixth form in September.

MARY MCGINTY: Er . . . No thank you, Mother. I'd rather not.

MOTHER THOMAS AQUINAS: I beg your pardon?

MARY MCGINTY: I'd rather leave school now, Mother Thomas.

MOTHER THOMAS AQUINAS: You can't possibly leave school now. You must get yourself qualified for some kind of job and maybe even acquire an A-level into the bargain.

MARY MCGINTY: I don't want to be a secretary, thank you, Mother.

MOTHER THOMAS AQUINAS: And what do you think you're going to be out in the world with no training of any kind and only the one solitary O-level to your name?

MARY MCGINTY: I might go and work in a shop.

MOTHER THOMAS AQUINAS: You didn't come to Our Lady of Fatima for five years to learn how to stand behind the counter of a shop, my dear girl.

MARY MCGINTY: Well, I wouldn't mind being a hairdresser.

MOTHER THOMAS AQUINAS: Jesus, Mary and Joseph, did you ever hear the like. A hairdresser.

MARY MCGINTY: Well the thing is, Mother, I'll probably be getting married quite soon.

MOTHER THOMAS AQUINAS: Indeed. Is this just wishful thinking? Or do you actually have a fiancé?

MARY MCGINTY: Yes, Mother.

MOTHER THOMAS AQUINAS: You have? At your age?

MARY MCGINTY: Yes, Mother.

MOTHER THOMAS AQUINAS: I take it he's a Catholic boy.

MARY MCGINTY: Er . . . not exactly, Mother. He might be changing his religion soon though.

MOTHER THOMAS AQUINAS: I see. Well, we can never have enough converts, that's for sure. But you can't possibly think of marriage for a long time yet. You'll have to go out and earn some sort of living. And you never know when you might need to help your husband support the children. What does the young man do for a living?

MARY MCGINTY: He's a Co-op milkman, Mother.

MOTHER THOMAS AQUINAS: Indeed.

MARY MCGINTY: But what he really wants to be is a train driver.

MOTHER THOMAS AQUINAS: Oh, take your head out of the clouds and come back down to earth, you silly girl. I'm certainly not going to accept your decision to leave school and go drifting into some dead-end job and wasting your life. And I'm sure your parents will be on my side. Be a good girl now and come back here in September and into the secretarial sixth form, even if it's only for the one year.

MARY MCGINTY: No, Mother. I don't want to.

MOTHER THOMAS AQUINAS: Never mind what you want or what you don't want. You'll do what I tell you to do.

MARY MCGINTY: No I won't. I don't have to. I'm leaving at the end of this term.

MOTHER THOMAS AQUINAS: Oh I think you'd better leave now, this minute, if that's how you're going to behave. Go on. Get out. Take your things home and don't bother coming back for the rest of the term. You think you know what's best for you, you don't want to be helped, well off you go then. And I hope you end up in the gutter.

MARY MCGINTY: [*jumping up and going to the door*] Yeah – and the same to you. You fucking old cunt.

> [MARY MCGINTY *runs away.* MOTHER THOMAS AQUINAS *makes the Sign of the Cross and says a silent prayer.* MARY MOONEY *comes in.*]

MOTHER THOMAS AQUINAS: Don't stand there gawping at me like an idiot. Well, I see you've done all right for yourself exam-wise. Not that there's any reason why you shouldn't have. You've brain enough inside your head. The question is, where do you go from here? Mr Emanuelli has told me you're keen to start studying singing full-time as soon as possible. He seems to think you have the vocal equipment for nothing less than the grand opera and I'm sure he knows about such things having been in the business himself. All I can say is you seem like a different girl altogether up on the stage, so maybe it'll be the makings of you. Now if you were any other girl with all these O-level passes I'd have no hesitation at all in sending you straight into the academic sixth form in September. But taking into account your past behaviour and keeping in mind that you're aiming for a musical career, I see no point at all in your remaining at this school. The best course of action for you, I should think, would be to go out and get yourself some little job which would leave you time enough for lessons with Mr Emanuelli. Unless of course your parents have any objections. Have you discussed your musical aspirations with them at any length?

MARY MOONEY: No, Mother Thomas.

MOTHER THOMAS AQUINAS: And for heaven's sake why not?

MARY MOONEY: I don't want to be a singer, Mother Thomas.

MOTHER THOMAS AQUINAS: But I spoke to Mr Emanuelli only yesterday and he was quite adamant ...

MARY MOONEY: I haven't told him yet, Mother Thomas.

MOTHER THOMAS AQUINAS: You let that poor man spend hours of his time instructing you and going to no end of trouble on your behalf and now you want to turn round and tell him he needn't have bothered. Oh, Mary Mooney, isn't that just like your impudence.

MARY MOONEY: I don't get on with him very well, Mother Thomas.

MOTHER THOMAS AQUINAS: Well, that's a fine thing to say when he has nothing but praise for you.

MARY MOONEY: I don't want to be left alone with him in his house, Mother Thomas. He's asked me to go there in the holidays.

MOTHER THOMAS AQUINAS: Indeed. It wouldn't be the first time you were alone with a man in his house, would it? [*She opens a drawer and brings out* MARY MOONEY'*s diary*.] At least not according to this diary of yours which you may have back but you needn't go looking for the two pages of obscenities because they've been ripped out and thrown into the boiler where they belong. You're on the right road to Hell, Mary Mooney.

MARY MOONEY: But I am still a virgin, Mother Thomas.

MOTHER THOMAS AQUINAS: Oh, be quiet! [*She takes a bible out of her desk*.] You may also take back the bible that you did not come forward to claim. I went through it very carefully indeed and besides finding several dubious passages underlined in pencil I also came across a Mass card for the soul of a certain Dominic Aloysius Mooney. You can be sure your sins will always find you out.

MARY MOONEY: Please, Mother Thomas, I ... I ...

MOTHER THOMAS AQUINAS: Well what is it? We haven't much time. Benediction will be starting in a minute.

MARY MOONEY: Please, Mother, I'd like to be a nun.

MOTHER THOMAS AQUINAS: Oh, would you now.

MARY MOONEY: Please, Mother, I've always wanted to be a nun. Ever since I was six years old.

MOTHER THOMAS AQUINAS: There was never a Catholic girl born that didn't want to be a nun at some stage of her developing years. But you're not a little girl now. You're a big girl with a great deal of experience. Go away now and be thankful you can sing for your supper.

MARY MOONEY: But, Mother, I have to be a nun. I want to be as perfect as I possibly can and be sure of getting a high place in Heaven.

MOTHER THOMAS AQUINAS: You haven't the necessary qualities, Mary Mooney. No. You're much more the type to go into show business.

MARY MOONEY: But, Mother, I want to give my voice back to Our Lord.

MOTHER THOMAS AQUINAS: What, fling it back in His face?

MARY MOONEY: No, Mother. Offer it up to Him by singing only for Him. Please, Mother, could you help me, please? I don't know who else I can go to.

MOTHER THOMAS AQUINAS: I can't believe a creature like you could possibly have a vocation. And I can't imagine what order would accept you. Certainly this one would not. Although, there again ... I don't know. I suppose we can't all be Maria Goretti. Don't you feel ashamed of yourself when you think of that wonderful virgin martyr?

MARY MOONEY: Yes, Mother Thomas.

MOTHER THOMAS AQUINAS: Saint Maria Goretti was only eleven years old when her purity was put to the test. In 1902. She too was left alone in a house with a man.

A great lout of a fellow who tempted her again and again but she would not give in to him. And when he found he could persuade her by no other means he threatened her with a shoemaker's awl. But still she would not commit a sin. She would not. So he got mad and took up the weapon and stabbed her with it no less than fourteen times. Mary Mooney, if you really think you have a vocation pray to Saint Maria Goretti for a positive sign. Now what about Mr Emanuelli? You'll have to tell him what you've just told me.

MARY MOONEY: Oh, I couldn't, Mother. I couldn't face him.

MOTHER THOMAS AQUINAS: Oh, but you'll have to. And I must have a word with your mother. Why does she never come near the school?

MARY MOONEY: She's always tired after work, Mother Thomas.

MOTHER THOMAS AQUINAS: What does your father do?

MARY MOONEY: Nothing, Mother. He's been retired for years.

MOTHER THOMAS AQUINAS: Is he a sick man?

MARY MOONEY: No, Mother. He's just old.

MOTHER THOMAS AQUINAS: Is he a great deal older than your mother?

MARY MOONEY: No, Mother. She's old too. She was nearly fifty when I was born. And now she's going to have another baby.

MOTHER THOMAS AQUINAS: Don't be so ridiculous. She can't be having a baby at that age.

MARY MOONEY: But she is, Mother. I know she is.

MOTHER THOMAS AQUINAS: If she is then she should be going into the *Guinness Book of Records*. Will you tell her to come and see me before the end of term?

MARY MOONEY: Yes, Mother Thomas.

MOTHER THOMAS AQUINAS: Go into the chapel. Kneel down in front of the crucifix and offer yourself body and soul to Our Blessed Lord who died for you.

MARY MOONEY: Yes, Mother Thomas.

MOTHER THOMAS AQUINAS: And this is your very last chance, Mary Mooney, I hope you realise. Your very last chance. Go along now.

MARY MOONEY: Yes, Mother Thomas. Thank you, Mother Thomas. Thank you very much indeed.

SCENE TEN

[*The Classroom.* MOTHER PETER *is at her desk.*]

MOTHER PETER: When you come back in September you may wear nylon stockings and a smart grey skirt instead of a gymslip. But don't let me see any sign of lipstick or bits of old jewellery. Apart from a holy medal or a crucifix. Those of you going out into the world must remember that the devil will be beckoning to you from every corner. But you can just tell him to go to Hell because you're not going to be fooled by him and his wily ways. You're going to show him a shining example of Christian purity. You may often be puzzled when you see decent young men hovering around young women who wear scanty clothes and say provocative things. But you can be sure that such women are really the object of those men's secret contempt. Oh yes indeed. Remember that God made your body for Himself. He lives in it and He may well want to use it for His own work later on when you marry, as a tabernacle for brand new life. All parts of the body are sacred but none more so than the parts connected with the mystery of motherhood. They should be treated with the greatest respect and guarded with absolute modesty. Scrupulous hygiene is, of course, vitally important and you need not imagine you are sinning when you sit in the bath and see yourself or touch yourself with the flannel. Just say a little prayer, think of Our Lady and remember that she had a body just like yours. Oh yes, and beware of indecent articles of news in what may otherwise appear to be innocent publications on sale in any shop. The *News of the World* is the one that springs most readily to mind. If you ever see the *News of the World* lying about on a bus or a train or in any public place don't hesitate to tear it up. And the very same applies to the *Daily Worker*. The rotten old rag of the Communists. Rip it into pieces. It's no easy task to live a good life in the adult world. We must take up our cross every day just like Our Blessed Lord and carry it with us wherever we go. And when God sends us any sickness or trouble we must accept it willingly and say 'Thy will be done. I take this for my sins.' And the best of luck to you. [*She makes the Sign of the Cross.*]

MOTHER PETER *and* GIRLS: In the name of the Father and of the Son and of the Holy Ghost, Amen.

Jesus, Mary and Joseph I give you my heart and my soul.

Jesus, Mary and Joseph assist me in my last agony.

Jesus, Mary and Joseph may I die in peace and in your blessed company. [*Sign of the Cross.*]

In the name of the Father and of the Son and of the Holy Ghost, Amen.

SCENE ELEVEN

[*The Back of the Chapel. A very large crucifix is hanging on the wall with candlesticks and a candle box by the side of it.* MARY MOONEY *comes in, genuflects in the direction of the altar and kneels down in front of the crucifix and prays.*]

VOICES OFF: [*singing*] 'Tantum ergo Sacramentum
　　　　Veneremur cernui:
　　　　Et antiquum documentum
　　　　Novo cedat ritui:
　　　　Praestet fides supplementum
　　　　Sensuum defectui.

　　　　Genitori Genitoque
　　　　Laus et jubilatio.
　　　　Salus, honor, virtus quoque
　　　　Sit et benedictio;
　　　　Procedenti ab utroque
　　　　Compar sit laudatio.
　　　　Amen.'

　　　　[MARY MOONEY *stands up, takes a candle, kisses it, blesses herself with it, lights it and puts it into a candlestick. Then she genuflects and goes off in the opposite direction to which she came in, walking backwards with her hands joined.*]

PRIEST: [*voice off, chanting*] 'Panem de caelo praestitisti eis. Alleluia.'

VOICES OFF: [*chanting*] 'Omne delectamentum in se habentem.'

　　　　[*Enter* MARY MCGINTY. *She genuflects in the direction of the altar, goes up to the crucifix and sticks something on it: a very long penis made of plasticine. She runs off.*]

PRIEST: [*voice off, speaking*] 'Oremus. Deus, qui nobis sub Sacramento mirabili passionis tuae memoriam reliquisti, tribue, quaesumus; ita nos Corporis et Sanguinis tui sacra mysteria venerari ut redemp-tionis tuae fructum in nobis jugiter sentiamus: qui vivis et regnas in saecula saeculorum. Amen.'

[*During the above prayer* MOTHER THOMAS AQUINAS *comes in. She genuflects, glances over at the crucifix, sees the plasticine penis and dashes over to remove it. Then she goes off in the opposite direction. She comes back holding* MARY MOONEY *by the scruff of the neck. They genuflect together in the direction of the altar then go off.*]

THE END